Praise for *The Power*

'*The Power of Connection* provides a
social connection in an increasingly   es
a practical guide to how to increase sc   ...s and social
skills. Dr Barry brings evolutionary scie ... and neuroscience into
the mix, providing an accessible and fascinating journey through
the brain and the relevance for social connections'

Professor Catherine Harmer, Professor of Cognitive
Neuroscience, University of Oxford

'*The Power of Connection* is another amazing book by the bestselling author Harry Barry. It is a book for everyone, beautifully
written, very accessible and readable. Drawing on his own clinical experience, neuroscience findings and practical exercises,
Dr Harry Barry offers us a deeper understanding of the world of
emotional connection, why it is important for us, and how it can
make us more resilient and better able to manage stress and the
challenges of life'

Sr Stanislaus Kennedy, social campaigner, author and founder of
Focus Ireland and the Sanctuary Meditation Centre

'It is an exceptionally wise book and, in true Dr Harry Barry style,
he doesn't simply stop at explaining the What and Why of meaningful human connection, he sets himself apart by teaching us the
HOW. Other books may enlighten you, but this book goes that
vital step further and turns information into knowledge with easy
tasks and thought exercises to help you build the relationships and
the life you want and deserve'

Stefanie Preissner, Sunday Independent *columnist, presenter of the
podcast* Basically . . .

'This handbook is essential for those seeking "a life well lived". Dr Barry is brilliant in his ability to explain challenges in growing strong bonds with others, be they social, with work colleagues, or in family and intimate relationships. His explanation of how our brains are built and function is one of the best I have come across. It conveys an overview, masterful in its breadth and comprehensiveness and the ease with which it can be understood. Whether a teen just exploring relationships, a twenty year old meeting turbulence in newly entered adult world, or an older person seeking to enrich life, this handbook will be of tremendous value'

Professor Larry Culpepper, Professor of Family Medicine,
Boston University School of Medicine

'At a time when social media means our world is both widely connected yet increasingly lonely, *The Power of Connection* challenges us to develop the skills to connect with each other at a one-to-one level. This timely book explores the wonders of our social brain, helps us understand the true importance of mastering skills such as empathy and conflict and brings the reader to a deeper understanding of themselves through self-acceptance, gratitude and kindness. Once again, Dr Barry brings us on a journey of discovery into how to connect with each other at a deeply human level. A book for our times'

Cathy Kelly, author and UNICEF ambassador

'Our connections with other people are crucial for our health and wellbeing – this book is an excellent practical guide to strengthening these'

Professor Ian Robertson, Professor of Psychology, Trinity College
Dublin, and author of How Confidence Works

THE POWER OF CONNECTION

CONNECTION

Change your relationships,
transform your life

DR HARRY BARRY

First published in Great Britain in 2023 by Orion Spring,
an imprint of The Orion Publishing Group Ltd
Carmelite House, 50 Victoria Embankment
London EC4Y 0DZ

An Hachette UK Company

1 3 5 7 9 10 8 6 4 2

Copyright © Dr Harry Barry 2023

The moral right of Dr Harry Barry to be identified as
the author of this work has been asserted in accordance
with the Copyright, Designs and Patents Act of 1988.

All rights reserved. No part of this publication may be
reproduced, stored in a retrieval system, or transmitted
in any form or by any means, electronic, mechanical,
photocopying, recording, or otherwise, without the
prior permission of both the copyright owner and the
above publisher of this book.

A CIP catalogue record for this book is
available from the British Library.

ISBN (Trade Paperback) 978 1 4091 9991 5
ISBN (eBook) 978 1 4091 9992 2
ISBN (Audio) 978 1 3987 0722 1

Typeset by Input Data Services Ltd, Bridgwater, Somerset

Printed and bound in Great Britain by Clays Ltd, Elcograf S.p.A.

MIX
Paper from
responsible sources
FSC® C104740
FSC
www.fsc.org

www.orionbooks.co.uk

I would like to dedicate this book to my dear friend Sr Stan Kennedy, founder of the homeless charity Focus Ireland and the Sanctuary, a meditation centre for social change. In a world so often filled with darkness and despair, she remains a constant beacon of light, hope, love and inspiration to us all

Every effort has been made to ensure that the information in this book is accurate. The information in this book may not be applicable in each individual case so it is advised that professional medical advice is obtained for specific health matters and before changing any medication or dosage. Neither the publisher nor author accepts any legal responsibility for any personal injury or other damage or loss arising from the use of the information in this book.

CONTENTS

PART FOUR – WEEK 3: HOW DO I INTERACT WITH OTHERS?

PART FIVE – WEEK 4: AM I CONFIDENT ENOUGH?

INTRODUCTION

There was something surreal about writing a book about the mysterious world of emotional connection, in the middle of a world-wide pandemic where the message emanating from authorities across the globe was a plea for all of us to stay as far apart from one another as possible. To avoid all of the social norms that have allowed us as human beings to survive and thrive over the aeons. It's a crisis that has also shown us the importance of face-to-face interpersonal communication in a manner that none of us could have predicted. It's become clearer than ever that human beings are social animals and we struggle to survive emotionally when forced to keep apart from one another.

Yet, long before this crisis, a major cultural change was already taking place. The arrival of technology, social media and the smartphone was beginning to intrude on those same critical interpersonal emotional connection skills which the pandemic has devastated. I had decided to write this book before the pandemic as I was increasingly concerned that we as a species are beginning to lose these essential life skills. This in turn was beginning to impact on our relationships at every level. I was especially uneasy about the long-term effects of this cultural change on our young people, who are not being tutored in these critical skills. I have also been interested in the importance of such skills in terms of emotional resilience and how their absence constitutes a major threat to our mental health and wellbeing. The more effectively we can truly connect with each other, the less likely we are to succumb to the three common forms of emotional distress, namely, anxiety, stress and depression.

The pandemic turned out to be a massive social experiment, with each one of us being asked to explore what life would really be like, if the necessity for normal human emotional connections were removed. The results have demonstrated how lonely life can become without them. How bland and uninteresting our world can suddenly seem. How emotionally barren and introverted we can become in the absence of such interpersonal communications, and how life can sometimes seem aimless and not worth living. The truth is that, as human beings, we are completely interdependent.

But why should this be the case? Why are these connections so important to us? The answer lies in the way in which we humans have evolved as a species. Our strength has always been our ability to emotionally connect with each other at multiple levels. It is this that has allowed us to grow and develop both individually and as a group. Those who develop their skills in these areas have an extraordinary advantage over those who lack them.

Perhaps you find yourself struggling with your capacity to emotionally connect with others? You may feel for example that you are not an effective communicator, or a good listener, or struggle with empathy or reading people, all of which are essential human skills. The good news is that it is never too late to learn. In reality, all of us can benefit from improving our skillset in this area. The promise of this book is that you can acquire such skills with the assistance of a simple four-week programme. You can change your life forever.

I hope you will join me on this journey of discovery.

PART ONE

BEFORE YOU BEGIN:

CONNECTIONS AND

UNDERSTANDING THE

BIOLOGY BEHIND THEM

1. Emotional Connection

Before the arrival of the computer, internet and social media, one of the most common ways of connecting with someone was through the world of business networking. Underlying this form of networking is the concept that business people are instinctively inclined to respond positively to those colleagues who have reached out to make a genuine connection with them. If both parties have areas of interest in common, outside of the workplace for example, then this bond increases the likelihood of reaching a deal in relation to business itself.

With the arrival of the internet and social media, the term networking then took on new meanings. Computer systems themselves are based on complex 'networks', which allow vast amounts of information to be stored and shared. This allowed a lot of networking to go online and, for many individuals and companies, revolutionized how business is carried out. The emergence of Facebook, Twitter, Instagram and LinkedIn etc. has further changed how we communicate with each other.

But, aside from these forms of networking, human beings since the beginning of their history have relied on a deeper, more meaningful form of communication with each other, namely, emotional connection.

What Is Emotional Connection?

Emotional connection relates to how we emotionally interact with each other at a one-to-one, face-to-face level. It involves a complex interactive set of skills that have the express aim of deepening and strengthening the emotional connections between us as human beings. Of all the skills that any of us can acquire for life, these are perhaps the most important because they are the key to successful personal relationships, fruitful social lives and being able to advance further down our chosen career path.

As a family doctor with over four decades of experience, I am often asked if someone's capacity for good emotional connection is inherent to the person. This concept, often attributed as well to the world of emotional resilience, is based on the idea that one is either resilient or an effective emotional communicator, or not, based on one's genes or family upbringing. I strongly reject this fixed view of both attributes. The reality is that we have been given one of the most powerful machines ever devised, to solve such issues, namely, the human brain. A dynamic organ that is, incredibly, designed to assist us in learning new skills and ideas. We will be reviewing the neuroscience of emotional connection later but, suffice to say, each one of us has an innate capacity to develop the necessary skills required to become a great emotional networker alongside the art of knowing how and when to use such skills. All that is needed is a belief that we as human beings can do so, together with an acceptance of the work necessary to develop them for life.

Why Is Emotional Connection Important for You?

Let's make this concept immediately more personal for you, the reader. Why is emotional connection important in your life? To answer this question, we must firstly take a look at the broader picture of the world in which you currently reside: a world obsessed with technology and social media.

Connecting with other people should be so simple, yet why do so many of us struggle socially? We live in a time where social media is rapidly becoming the dominant medium through which we communicate with each other. People are reaching out via social media for company, companionship and human connection, but frequently discovering that this form of networking leaves them feeling even more disconnected. This makes sense, as it's emotional connections that human beings require most, and social media often fails to satisfy that need.

Many of us assume, for example, that connecting or networking with large numbers of people online, known as social networking, means that we are effective emotional connectors in the real world. Alas nothing could be further from the truth. True emotional connection involves genuine face-to-face communication skills. Many of us struggle with these skills, as they do not form part of our current educational system, and this can result in multiple difficulties in relation to different aspects of our daily life. How often have you struggled for example to emotionally connect with someone sitting beside you at a dinner party? Or struggled to smooth over a difficult conversation with a family member or colleague? Perhaps you can recognize yourself in this space and would love to become a genuine emotional connector.

Here's a list of some of the many ways that improving your emotional connection skills can change your life.

Imagine if you could:

- easily relate to others and be at ease in any social or professional situation in which you find yourself
- be someone towards whom others instantly gravitate, sensing that you are someone they will feel comfortable being with
- have the skills necessary to emotionally connect with others in multiple different life situations
- have the attributes necessary to become more connected to family, friends, relationships and society in general
- become more empathetic and socially connected with others
- become a kinder, warmer, more fulfilled person
- become more effective in the workplace.
- be increasingly successful and enriched in your everyday personal relationships and experience deeper friendships
- improve your romantic relationships, find love more easily in your life, and become better equipped to navigate difficult family or other relationships
- live in a world where you are less likely to be lonely and more genuinely 'connected'.

Imagine the positive effects of all of this on your mental and physical health. How enriched your life could become if you could develop such skills.

These are the rewards for working hard on improving your emotional connection techniques. The real question is, 'Can you afford not to do so?' Over decades of assisting those with mental health difficulties, it has become increasingly clear to me that those who develop such skills become more resilient and cope better with common mental health problems such as stress, anxiety and depression. I have also seen those who have worked on and improved their emotional connection skills cope better with many of the trials that life will inevitably send us.

Emotional Connection and Your Mental Health

One could justifiably ask 'Why are emotional connection skills so important for your mental health?' This is an important question and one of great relevance to those of us who work in this area. While it makes sense that good emotional connection skills will be of great benefit in improving the quality and effectiveness of your personal and social relationships, and working life, it may be less clear as to why such skills are of relevance to your overall mental health and wellbeing.

There is much talk nowadays about the importance of our mental health and wellbeing. How self-care is rising increasingly to the surface as being critical to our capacity to stay mentally well. There is increasing interest for example in the importance of sleep, exercise, nutrition, work/life balance and mindfulness in relation to self-care. Maybe the time has come to add emotional connection skills to this list, for those who have acquired such skills are less likely to get into difficulties with their mental health and wellbeing.

Let us look at one of the commonest conditions of all, namely stress. Many of us become incredibly stressed over interpersonal relationship difficulties, as many couples can attest to. A great number of these situations are blighted by an absence of good emotional communication skills such as empathy and active listening. Similarly, family, friendship, and working dynamics can put huge stress on your internal coping mechanisms. Good effective emotional connection techniques often circumvent the issues involved in such situations.

One of the common difficulties faced by those who suffer from acute, general and especially social anxiety is an inability to effectively communicate with others as to the difficulties that the sufferer is experiencing. The more we improve our communication skills, the easier it becomes to seek out effective treatment options, which can so benefit those struggling with such conditions. Social anxiety for example (as we will explore later) is one of those conditions where a lack of understanding of what genuine emotional connection is all about can lead to the person in question living a life of quiet hell.

Those undergoing bouts of clinical depression often find emotional communications especially difficult, both during those hard times and when in remission. This makes sense, as this illness really disrupts and distorts many of the communication systems that we all use on a daily basis to link in and connect with each other. This can lead to the person with this condition feeling increasingly isolated and lonely. This is why it is so key that they too work on their emotional connection skills once the bout in question has been treated appropriately.

There are some other groups for whom normal emotional connection can also be especially challenging. The largest by far are those who are on the ASD spectrum. This is because they, for neuroscientific reasons, are hard-wired to misread, or struggle to grasp, many of the subtle cues so crucial for such networking. It does not mean that emotional connection is not possible for them, it just has to be taught using different approaches.

The Role of Emotional Connection in Preparing Our Young People for Life

I have spoken and written at length about the importance of preparing our children, adolescents and young adults for life by ensuring that they are taught relevant emotional resilience skills. How, despite the best efforts of both parents and educators, many are entering adult life less prepared than one would like for the harsh realities that they may have to face.

We rarely discuss the importance of emotional connection when exploring the skills they will require to survive and thrive. Do we for example equip them with the appropriate listening and conversational skills, so vital for their future social interactions? How to be more aware of non-verbal cues? Improve their people-to-people skills by teaching them to become more empathetic, read people and manage conflict? Or strengthen their personal skills by teaching them the importance of self-acceptance, kindness and compassion when communicating with others?

The answer to these questions is in general, sadly, no. Very few of our adolescents and young adults are ever really taught these essential techniques and skills. They are of course experts in all areas of social networking based on technology and social media. But this has not prevented them alas from encountering a tsunami of mental health difficulties such as anxiety, depression, eating disorders and self-harm. If adolescents were taught human face-to-face communication skills from the outset, and encouraged to introduce them into every facet of their young adult lives, I believe this would make a huge difference. But, perhaps, we adults must firstly learn how to apply these techniques in our *own* lives before sharing them with our young people. Hopefully this book will assist you in doing just that.

The Importance of Emotional Connection for Companies

Increasingly, large businesses and companies are beginning to appreciate the importance of emotional connection at an individual and corporate level. There has always been an acceptance of the importance of networking as a concept, with the social media world being the most recent vehicle for its usage. Now, at last, there is an understanding that true emotional communication must go much deeper.

It is no longer a question of how many networking connections you have built up, but rather the depth and quality of those connections at a human and personal level, which may decide how effective you are, both individually and as a company.

There is also an increasing acceptance that good interpersonal emotional connection skills harmonize working relationships, improve overall efficiency and, most of all, protect the mental health of those involved. There will be a high price to be paid in terms of stress, anxiety, depression, absenteeism and presenteeism, when such skills are not developed and strengthened at a corporate level.

Emotional Connection: Conscious or Subliminal?

What many of us fail to recognize is how much work our brain does unconsciously every moment of our lives. This is one of the major reasons human beings have been able to advance so quickly over the past ten thousand years. If we had to focus attention on every detail involved in walking from the kitchen to the bedroom, or eating a meal, or driving the car to work, for example, there would be little time or space left for anything else in our lives. The reality is that the brain has evolved to unconsciously carry out such functions. We do not have to worry about our heart pumping, our breathing or balance – it quietly performs such functions without any input from our conscious selves.

It is therefore appropriate to inquire whether emotional connection is a conscious or a subliminal or unconscious process. This question is critical if we hope to improve our skills in this area. The answer is that it is a hybrid of both. The vast majority of our communication happens subliminally or unconsciously, but there is still an active role for our rational or conscious brain in the process. There is also a significant and complex interaction between our conscious and unconscious systems, and it is this interaction that we will be harnessing when developing our skills in this area.

As we will see later, skills often require an active or conscious input when learning and developing them but can be transferred to lower levels of consciousness when we have mastered them. It would be my hope for you that, by the end of this book, most of your emotional connection will occur subliminally and naturally, freeing you up to really enjoy the fruits of your hard work in developing the skills and arts required.

Emotional Connection: A Skill or an Art?

Very few of us are 'born' with a built-in aptitude for emotional connection in our social world. Rather, as we will be exploring further, it is possible to become a powerful emotional connector, by learning and developing a suite of critical communication and personal skills. But even if we possess some of these skills, we often fail to understand when and how best to use them. Improving your emotional connection skills is therefore not just about learning skills but learning how to use them effectively; it is both a skill and an art.

In the course of this book we therefore will have to firstly understand and learn the skills required and then practise them in our everyday lives. It is only then, through a process of observing how their application in practice works, that we slowly but surely develop the art of emotional connection. We will see this play out in practice later in this book.

The practice of medicine is similar in nature. Most doctors spend many years building up a raft of clinical skills, which they learn to put into practice over subsequent decades. It takes much longer however to learn the art of medicine. This will often include knowing when and where to use the clinical skills that one has built up. It involves learning to trust one's instincts in certain situations (often based on years of face-to-face consultations) while still rooting decisions in solid clinical foundations. This is what we mean by the art of medicine: the ability to know how best to use the skills that we have built up over time, to achieve the best outcomes for the patient.

What Are Soft Skills?

In a modern world obsessed with science, engineering, technology and social media, hard skills such as problem-solving and the management of technical, organizational, behavioural and business difficulties have been those most sought after. These include science, mathematics, understanding algorithms, business management, problem-solving, and a whole host of similar skills.

It is easy however to overlook the importance of soft skills. The term 'soft' suggests that these skills are of less relevance than the colder, more logic-based harder skills. The reality of course is that soft skills such as listening, non-verbal cues, empathy and people-to-people interactional skills are perhaps more important tools to have in your toolkit, if you wish to be successful in many areas of life.

As technology subtly invades every aspect of our lives, these soft skills will become increasingly important in how we relate to each other. Those who take the time and effort to attain them, will often find themselves forging ahead faster in all domains of their lives.

What About the Written Word?

Clearly networking can involve a number of different mediums outside direct face-to-face communication. We can communicate through the written word, music, the arts and, nowadays through mediums such as texting and social media in all its constantly changing forms. To explore the role of all of these forms of communication or networking in any detail is beyond the scope of this book, which hopes to explore instead the nuances of face-to-face networking. However, it is worth briefly exploring the written word, which has played such an important role in how we have communicated and networked with each other throughout the ages.

While human beings have been communicating with each other verbally for over 200,000 years, it was not until 4,000 years BC that the written word or writing came into being, probably originating in Mesopotamia. We have come a long way from human beings communicating with each other through the written word through etchings on stone tablets in Sumeria BC to where we are today. The arrival of the printing press in the fifteenth century revolutionized the nature of the written word, allowing us to disseminate information more efficiently and to a larger audience.

I would like to pick out one particular form of communication or networking that I believe still has the power to affect us deeply at an emotional level: the humble letter (especially if written by hand). The more we have evolved to lead our lives through the mediums of technology and social media, the more this form of communication has been pushed to one side. This is a tragedy, as there is something special about opening up our hearts to each other in a letter, which will always remain a uniquely human form of emotional networking.

It is perhaps the only real form of the written word that comes close to the face-to-face networking that will form the basis of this book. This is because it takes time, effort, thought and often a conscious decision to truly open up to how we are feeling. But also to empathize with where the recipient of the letter might be emotionally at that moment in time. One of the advantages of such letters is that we have time to pause and reflect on what we want to say, rather than the instant forms of networking so prevalent in our modern society.

It is my hope that you too may also recognize the power of the handwritten letter to emotionally network or connect with those you value the most. Many of the skills that assist us to become good face-to-face networkers are necessary to become skilled at writing such letters. If you can work on this skill and add it to becoming an effective face-to-face emotional networker, your life will become much the richer.

Emotional Connection vs Social Media

Before leaving our discussion on emotional connection, it's important to explore its role in the new world of social media. Social media allied to the creation of the smartphone represents the greatest advance in how we communicate with each other, since the arrival of the printing press, discussed earlier.

Mark Zuckerberg launched Facebook in 2004 and, since its arrival, the world has never been the same again. Facebook was based on the concept that people would put up content about themselves and that others would then decide to 'like' their input, or not. Facebook is now an international tech giant and its founder an extremely wealthy man. Around the same time, Google and Twitter were also launched, the former in 1998 and the latter in 2006. These companies have grown to be the dominant forces in our lives, transforming how we communicate with each other. Information is the new currency and these companies have made fortunes by harvesting our personal data. They are controlling much of what we think, believe and do, often subconsciously.

At the same time as these three giant corporations were exponentially growing, we also experienced the arrival of the modern smartphone. Acting not only as a routine mobile phone, it also allows us instant access to the internet, emails, text messaging, sat nav, video games, a camera and videos, amongst multiple other functions. It is difficult to comprehend that the first modern version was only launched in 2000.

When we combine the modern smartphone with social media, we would seem to have the perfect networking system in place. If we combine the power of the larger social-media platforms such as Facebook and Twitter, where people are encouraged to share every personal moment of their lives with others, and add in newer platforms such as Instagram, a photo and video-sharing social-networking service launched in 2010, Snapchat, a multimedia messaging app launched in 2011, and most recently TikTok, with the modern smartphone, it would appear that routine emotional connection is on the road to extinction. How could human beings communicating face to face with each other ever hope to compete with the networking monster created by social media and the smartphone?

This is an important discussion and one that each of us individually and as a society need to have. Of course, technology and social media have major benefits and add much to our lives. They have enormous value. They are essential for connectivity, research, health, policing, business, marketing and education, amongst their many applications. The world is rapidly becoming a 'virtual global village'.

There are significant downsides however to allowing technology and social media to become the dominant force in our lives. One of the major casualties is emotional connection. As we will be exploring in this book, this is best done in face-to-face encounters, where all the nuances of verbal and non-verbal communication are laid bare. It is difficult, well-nigh impossible, to gain the wealth of information that the social brain picks up during such encounters, while communicating through these other mediums.

The Covid pandemic in 2019 led many of us to see the reality of what the world would look like if all communications between human beings was switched overnight to being virtual. In many ways it has highlighted the dilemma that faces us all.

On the one hand technology, social media and the smartphone turned out to be our saviour in allowing us to communicate with each other at an individual, family, community and corporate level, through mediums like Zoom, Teams, FaceTime and WhatsApp. It assisted many workplaces, for example, to continue business almost as normal, allowed significant numbers to work from home and was invaluable in helping families to stay in contact with each other, even at long distances. It was especially important for those who were forced to self-isolate or shield due to age or vulnerability and for those who lived on their own. It was also of great assistance in allowing family members to say goodbyes to loved ones dying of Covid in ICUs.

On the other hand, the continuous usage of such virtual platforms exhausted us all, often leaving us strangely unfulfilled and detached. It was as if we were all in individual bubbles, communicating, but not really emotionally connecting, with each other. Zoom-fatigue became the buzzword of the pandemic. Many of us grew to intensely dislike those artificial social occasions, where family or friends tried to meet up online. Workers grew to hate the constant stream of online Zoom meetings. Burnout became almost ubiquitous. Our stress systems simply could not cope with the non-stop virtual world barrage, in the absence of real human contact.

What was missing of course was the emotional impact of those face-to-face encounters, which make up so much of our daily lives. Those spontaneous encounters at the water cooler, the coffee machine, the local supermarket, pub or post office, all of which allow us the opportunity to truly communicate and network with each other. Where we could listen and converse naturally, pick up all those non-verbal cues and show and receive empathy. Where we could nourish each other through such natural human contact. Where we could really interact at a deeper level than through any virtual platform.

Clearly there is a critical message here. As human beings we have to find new ways to integrate these two forms of communication or networking into our lives. We cannot exclude one or the other. Both have an important role to play. The pandemic has demonstrated, however, the importance of genuine face-to-face communication and the advantages of becoming skilled in this area. Those who did have these skills, seemed to cope better even in the virtual artificial world created during the crisis. They will also find it easier to re-socialize over the months and years that will follow this pandemic.

Our Four-Week Programme

Now that we've outlined *why* emotional connections are critical for our good health and wellbeing, it's time to look at *how* we can develop this life-changing skill.

You may assume that achieving this goal is going to take a considerable amount of time and effort, and be put off by this thought.

If this is a concern for you, then please don't worry. I have put together a simple four-week programme that will allow you to quickly and efficiently improve your expertise in this area. Let's explore this programme in greater detail.

In this book, we will explore the four important strategic groups that relate to improving our emotional connections. These are:

1. Verbal Strategies
2. Non-verbal Strategies
3. People-to-People Strategies
4. Personal Development Strategies

Within each of these strategic areas, we will then dive into specific skills (and relevant exercises that you can complete) to improve your proficiency in the area. For example:

1. Verbal Strategies skill: how to listen
2. Non-verbal Strategies skill: how to make eye contact
3. People-to-People Strategies skill: how to improve your empathy

4. Personal Development Strategies skill: how to be yourself in social situations

In our four-week programme then, I will ask you to pick one skill from each of the four strategic areas, preferably ones you find yourself struggling with most. You'll find a list of the skills covered in each strategy at the start of the section. Each week you will then practise one specific skill, and so your month-long programme might therefore look like this:

Week	Strategic area	Chosen skill
1	Verbal	How to listen
2	Non-verbal	How to make eye contact
3	People-To-People	How to improve your empathy
4	Personal Development	How to be yourself in social situations

By the end of week four, you will have hopefully mastered four skills, one from each group. If you feel that you need more time to master them, then simply repeat the four-week programme for a second time or until you are comfortable applying them to your life. You choose your own pace to proceed. Most of you will probably feel that you have a good grasp of the four skills in question by the end of the four-week period.

If you feel comfortable that you have mastered these four skills, you might decide to then advance to picking four new skills, again one from each grouping, and applying them weekly for another four weeks. In this way, you will quickly build up a compendium of critical emotional connection skills, which will transform your life for good.

All going well, by applying our four-week programme in this manner, at the end of a twelve-week period you'll have learned twelve new emotional connection skills and become a more skilled emotional communicator.

How to Use This Book

There are a number of ways to read this book. You could decide to get a complete overview of the four strategic areas outlined on p.20 before taking action with the four-week plan. If so, then read this book as it has been laid out and only then begin to apply the programme, detailed above.

On the other hand, you may feel you want to begin the four-week programme immediately or in tandem with reading the book as a whole, and this too is fine. In which case, as you finish reading about each strategic area, choose a skill to focus on that week.

The most important thing is that you feel comfortable with whatever decision you make. My advice, whichever route you choose, is to always pick four skills that you are currently struggling with, as this will give you great confidence going forward. It is also ideal to choose one skill from each of the four strategic areas as they all complement one another well and will ensure you become a rounded communicator.

You may feel quite comfortable in reading about and applying many of the skills and techniques laid out in this book. If, however, you feel that working with a life coach or therapist would be of assistance, then I would recommend doing just that. If you are also experiencing any conditions such as anxiety or depression, you may be more comfortable accessing help from your family doctor or a therapist for these conditions first, before embarking on the emotional connection skills laid out in this book. Once again, I would counsel you to do just that.

Before advancing to explore the four main strategic groups in greater detail and how to acquire the necessary emotional connection skills, let's first examine the neuroscience of how we make connections as human beings. This understanding is vitally important, as it underlies many of the techniques laid out in this book.

2. Your Social Brain

The social brain underlies many of the vital processes involved in how we emotionally interconnect with each other. These include listening, conversing, reading non-verbal cues and a whole host of other interpersonal and personal skills. It is this engine that we will be tapping into, as we explore the magical world of emotional connections.

Your social brain is the engine of emotional connection and yet we rarely stop to consider just how important it is in this whole process. Paradoxically, making connections is how the brain itself works and, while it might be hard to believe, by the time you read to the end of this chapter, your brain, by absorbing the information it contains, will have literally reshaped some of its connections and pathways. This is a process called neuroplasticity, which we will be discussing further on.

You may be tempted to skip this chapter, but I would strongly advise you not to do so. It is critically important to understand why all of us behave the way we do in social situations, because so much of what happens in social interactions is unconscious and our social brain is central to this process. A better understanding of the science behind the biological connections happening in your body will greatly enrich your understanding of the world of emotional connection, and the power of the brain to focus consciously on what is routinely an unconscious process. This understanding lies at the heart of this book.

The Neuroscience of Emotional Connection

It is helpful from the outset to understand how your social brain networks function. What are the key players in the brain and how do they interact with each other under normal social circumstances? Are there brain networks specific to social interactions and how do they work? Understanding such networks is important, as they shed some light on why you may struggle to connect in some situations and not in others. We will be mentioning some of these systems throughout the book, so it is useful to have some insight into how they are laid out in your brain.

I am going to summarize some of the key neuroscience findings relevant to our discussion on the links between your social brain and emotional networking.

We will begin by examining the role of two significant players in the brain, which are key to how you understand your social world.

1. The first structure, situated at the front of the brain, is called the prefrontal cortex (PFC), and is the thinking, sensible, rational (to a point), problem-solving part of the brain, often described as the logical brain.
2. The second structure, situated in the middle of the brain, is called the limbic system. Alongside monitoring vital bodily functions, one of its primary functions is to oversee

your emotional world, which is why it is frequently referred to as the emotional brain.

Within both structures are key sections, which play a vital role in how you interpret your social world and interact within it. Let's explore these in greater detail.

The Prefrontal Cortex (PFC)

Human beings have a right and left PFC, which have broadly different functions. The left PFC is more geared towards language, problem-solving and more positive emotions, motivations and actions. Your right PFC is more geared towards handling your emotional world, especially negative emotions such as fear, anxiety and depression, and also towards negative avoidant behaviours. It is also the source of your natural human tendency to catastrophize.

Those of us who find ourselves more anxious in general, or particularly in social situations, may tend to work more out of our right hemisphere, tending to see the more negative aspects of such situations. They may also tend to catastrophize and avoid social situations more than others. They therefore may struggle more with emotional networking, but will also benefit greatly from working on developing skills and learning how best to improve them.

Those people who struggle more with bouts of clinical depression may on the other hand find that their left PFC is underactive, so may find it harder to access positive emotions or to motivate themselves in social situations. They are more prone to picking up negative vibrations in social situations and to judging themselves accordingly as of lesser value or consequence.

The left PFC is often seen as the 'fine detail' hemisphere, whereas the right PFC is more about the 'broader canvas' of life. In everyday life, because both are strongly interconnected, the two sides work smoothly together.

The PFC can be broken down into four main sections, all of which are of relevance to our discussion:

1. The dorsal prefrontal cortex
2. The orbitofrontal cortex
3. The ventromedial cortex
4. The anterior cingulate cortex

Let's take a look at each of these in turn.

The Dorsal Prefrontal Cortex (DPFC)

This is the 'boss' of both the brain and of us as individuals. We have one on each side of the brain. When logically analysing situations, planning strategies, focusing conscious attention on thoughts, emotions and behaviour, deciding on 'options', meditating, problem-solving or reasoning, this part of the brain is buzzing. The right DPFC is associated with creativity/visual imagery, the left with the hard-nosed decision-making of everyday lives and concepts involving language and planning. This is the part of the rational brain that will sometimes balance out or even override social conclusions we make during networking and the subsequent actions we might take as a result.

The Orbitofrontal Cortex (OFC)

This is now seen as one of the most important parts of the brain in relation to how we socially and emotionally network. We have one on both sides of the brain, situated over our eye orbits, from which it gets its name. It is seen as the boss or controller general of our internal and external social world and how we react to social situations and is thus a key player in emotional networking. It is considered one of the most likely neural sources of empathy, which is a critical skill in how we communicate and one that we will be exploring later. It may even control our unique capacity to 'sense' where people we meet are, from an emotional point of view – now seen as the basis of empathy.

It also assists us in deferring immediate gratification and suppressing emotions for longterm gain. It makes sense of our social world, making lightning-fast assessments of people we encounter, and deciding whether we face or withdraw from particular social situations. Do we like or dislike someone we meet in such situations? How should we behave as a result? These feelings and decisions as we will see are often made at lightning speeds, and it is this part of the brain that controls both.

The OFC is also in constant communication with the amygdala, the boss of our emotional world (which we will be discussing in the next section), dampening down emotional surges and impulses. There has been considerable interest in assessing its role in behaviour. When the OFC is malfunctioning, we lack motivation and behavioural control. We know for example that in psychopaths this part of the brain is malfunctioning, often underactive.

The Ventromedial Cortex (VMPFC)
This area of the prefrontal cortex monitors emotions, deciding when, if and how they should be modified, and the appropriate emotional behavioural responses. Together with the OFC it assists us in regulating our emotions in social situations, making appropriate decisions and judgement calls during them. It also assists us in seeing the bigger picture.

The Anterior Cingulate Cortex (ACC)

This is the part of our brain that links our logical and emotional worlds together. Some regard it as the 'meeting point' between the information flowing up from our unconscious emotional limbic system and the conscious, logical, more rational areas of the pre-frontal cortex. Known functions include information-processing, attention, focused problem-solving, and the expression and modulation of emotion (emotional self-control).

When we are well, the ACC makes sense of our inner emotional world, ensuring a healthy 'analysis' of how an emotion is affecting us, and ensuring that our rational mind can assess whether such emotions are appropriate. In other words, it allows us to rationalize our emotions. The more activated the ACC is, the calmer and more 'sensible' emotional responses will be. There is increased functioning in individuals with greater social insight and maturity and higher levels of social awareness.

There are powerful connections between our ACC and our OFC and between our ACC and the amygdala, and these are key pathways in relation to how we emotionally network with each other.

The Limbic System

There are three key sections in your emotional brain that are of relevance to your social world. These are:

1. The amygdala
2. The hippocampus
3. The insular cortex

Again, let's take a look at these parts of the limbic system in more detail.

The Amygdala

This is the most important part of your emotional brain, which relates to your social world. You have one on both sides of the brain. It controls responses to perceived threats both within the body and in the external environment, which is why it is a key player in panic attacks and phobias. It is the main processor of the primary emotions of fear, hate, love and anger. It assists your brain in storing emotions related to unpleasant memories, which may or may not be consciously accessible. It plays a role in your assessment of facial expressions. By misreading other people's facial expressions, as in social anxiety or depression for example, it can unleash a stream of negative emotional thoughts and behaviours.

The amygdala is also in charge of your stress system. It has long been recognized that this primitive but immensely powerful part of the brain is key to how we emotionally react to each other in social situations. Thankfully it is strongly monitored by the OFC, with inputs from other parts of the rational brain. This allows us to modulate our emotional responses while communicating or networking with each other.

The Hippocampus

This is where your memory is manufactured, filtered and retrieved and also where these recalled memories are put into context. It should be seen as the central sorting agency for your memories, so will play a major role in how we network with each other. It is often said that we as human beings are our memories, and there is much truth in this statement. The hippocampus is situated close to the amygdala with good reason. The hippocampus stores the context of your memories, while the amygdala stores the emotions generated by the same occurrence.

Let's suppose you are networking with a close friend whom you have met while out walking in your local park. Your hippocampus will take in all of the details of that moment, your surroundings, sounds of the birds, the smell of cut grass, details about your friend, what she was wearing and so on. The reason that you recognize your friend in the first place is because previous memories of her are retrieved instantly and seamlessly slotted into your consciousness. The amygdala will store your emotional reaction to meeting your friend, the sense of joy and happiness generated by the meeting and so on.

These memories are consolidated while you sleep and stored away in different parts of the brain, with the hippocampus able to retrieve them in the future as required. Every time you retrieve a memory from the hippocampus and use it, that memory is subtly altered. A good analogy is retrieving a computer file, opening, reading it, adding some relevant data to the file, saving it and returning it to its original storage area. The same process occurs when you access emotional memories with the help of the amygdala. In the example above, your hippocampus might add in new details such as the fact that your friend seems to have lost some weight while your amygdala might trigger some undeclared emotions of anxiety as to why this might be the case.

It is extraordinary that all of this dance is going on unconsciously as you are greeting your friend and connecting with them. Sadly, only when your hippocampus begins to degenerate in conditions such as Alzheimer's disease do we really begin to understand the importance of this organ.

The Insular Cortex (Insula)

Studies suggest that the insular cortex plays an important role in processing social emotions like pride, guilt, humiliation, lust,

disgust and, in particular, empathy. It is also involved in the antici-
pation and feeling of physical and emotional pain and the ability
to share in another person's feelings of pain. We have one organ
on each side of the brain, which receives information from the
skin and internal organs. There is a crucial part at the front of
the insula in humans that reinterprets these sensations as social
emotions – a bad odour is translated into the emotion of disgust, a
caress into a feeling of loving warmth, and so on. The right insula
is more active in this transformation. This is where you sense love
and hate, resentment, embarrassment, trust and distrust, pride
and humiliation, guilt, deception, and so on.

The insula has particularly strong connections with the OFC,
forming the basis of your empathy pathways. It also liaises closely
with the amygdala and is a major player in the world of the emotions. It thus plays an important role in our social world and how
we empathize, socially connect and bond with each other, all critical elements of emotional networking.

The Major Social Brain Networks

Apart from the above structures there are two internal neural networking systems that play a major role in the social brain and are
intrinsic to how we emotionally network with each other.

The Spindle Cell Network

Every moment of the day as human beings we are making
lightning-fast social interactional decisions, many of which are
happening subliminally or unconsciously. To facilitate these
networking interactions, the brain has evolved a unique set of
specialized brain cells or neurons, which are called spindle cells.
These cells are so called as they are shaped like a spindle and they
are four times as large as routine neurons in the brain. They are

so designed to be able to transmit information at incredibly fast speeds. They are even structured differently to other nerve cells in the brain. These cells have been created with the primary task of connecting the key structures involved in our social brain in such a way that we can assess social situations quickly and, if necessary, make the appropriate actions in them. We will show how this would work in practice later.

Spindle cells are especially abundant in some of the structures mentioned already as key players in your social world, namely the OFC, the ACC and the insula (see above), especially in the right brain, but their extensive connections spread right across the whole brain, so they play a major role in our busy lives, even if we are totally unaware of their existence. Some areas of the OFC, activated during your emotional reactions to others, are especially rich in spindle cells. These are strongly activated for example when you experience an immediate emotional empathy bond with another person.

It could be said that it is this system of brain connections which defines our species as human beings, as we are the only one with such a rich supply of these extraordinary nerve cells, dwarfing our nearest relatives the great apes by a thousand times their number. For it is our ability to socially and emotionally network with each other that has allowed us as human beings to advance so quickly over the past ten thousand years.

Spindle neurons play a role in how you react emotionally to others (love, hate, like, dislike), and in coordinating your emotional, behavioural and social pathways in the brain, so clearly they are going to be key players in emotional networking.

If, however, so much of the work of this system is happening subconsciously, subliminally and at breakneck speed, one might ask how we can hope to improve or change how we emotionally network. Amazingly, however, we do have the ability to reshape both our neural pathways and indeed our thinking and behavioural patterns to achieve this objective. I hope to explore how you can do just this as we progress through this book.

The Mirror Neuron Network

One of the most important discoveries in our understanding of the modern human brain was made in 1992 by Italian researchers studying the brain of a particular monkey. They noticed that the monkey, when observing one of their team eating an ice-cream cone, showed evidence of brain activity as if it had been performing the same function, even though it was not. On further investigation, they identified special neurons in the human brain, which they called 'mirror neurons' – so called because they allow us to 'mirror', or reflect back, observed actions of others. We have multiple mirror neuron systems in the human brain. They can be activated by observing another person performing an action, or even when we anticipate that someone will perform such an action. This has profound implications for how we as human beings learn from each other, and researchers are still unravelling the multiple functions of this amazing system. When reading a book, for example, our mirror neurons keep imitating what we read. If the characters in the book perform different actions, mirror neurons fire as if doing the same. Similarly, on hearing certain sounds, mirror neurons in our language centres will build a picture of what they actually represent.

Mirror neurons are also strongly activated in social interactions, particularly in our OFC and during empathy experiences. Empathy mirror neurons allow us to pick up on emotions from each other, creating an internal picture of the other person's emotions and feelings as if we are experiencing them ourselves. We do this by absorbing information from facial expressions, listening to the other person's speech, watching their actions and behaviour, and so on. All the while, our mirror neurons activate as if it was us talking and acting. We can strongly influence each other through this system, as it forms part of the empathy experience. This is why if we meet a person who is positive and upbeat, they seem to influence us and we often find ourselves feeling better about ourselves. Similarly, if someone is negative or angry and bitter, that also 'rubs off' on us. We are most influenced for the better, as we will discuss later in the book, by those who love and accept themselves and others without condition. Through empathy and our mirror neuron system, we therefore can become nourished and positive in their presence.

Some people have a more highly developed mirror system than others in relation to empathy. Women seem more highly tuned in this area, due to their greater brain connectivity. The better we are at this internal 'mind reading', the more socially adept and comfortable we are, and vice versa. It is also one of the traits of the better therapists. From a positive perspective, it is probably this system that allows us to be comfortable in the presence of a therapist we trust. It is a meeting of two mirror systems: a brain-to-brain passage of emotional information from one human being to another. We begin to build a new picture of ourselves through this social interaction. Initially it was thought that perhaps those on the autism spectrum who struggle with picking up on emotional cues might have a malfunctioning mirror neuron system, but this has not been borne out through research.

Your Social Brain in Action

We have now explored the neuroscience behind how your social brain's structures and networks are set up to assist you to emotionally network. It is useful to see how this might play out in practice in a normal social situation, such as when Simon, who is quite shy and socially anxious, meets Sue at a party in their local pub.

Simon's Story
Simon enters the party feeling extremely anxious. His amygdala, sensing his unease, activates his stress system to pump out copious amounts of his fear hormone adrenaline, so he is shaking, sweating and extremely fidgety. His instinctive thought is to turn on his heels and leave the party, before matters get worse and he is forced to interact socially with people whom he has never met before, especially if female. But he decides to head initially to the bar for a pint, to calm down his symptoms of anxiety. Maybe this would be of assistance, but he is unaware of the fact that the alcohol has encouraged his brain to release small chemical messengers into his brain such as dopamine and GABA, which have the effect of temporarily calming down his amygdala.

At the bar he encounters a work colleague whom he has never got on with. He has never really understood why this was the case. But unconsciously his OFC and insula were picking up some information from his colleague. Firstly, his colleague's body language, which is unconsciously being registered by Simon's internal social monitoring system, is contradicting his seeming friendly overtures. Secondly, his colleague has always exuded an unpleasant body odour, which Simon's insula finds repellent. Thirdly, Simon constantly struggles to build up any positive empathy bond with this particular colleague, who seems only interested in talking about himself. All of this information is being absorbed and assessed with the assistance of his spindle and mirror neuron systems, OFC, ACC and insula, adding to the pressure already being exerted by his amygdala. As a result, Simon decides to finish his drink as quickly as possible and make his exit, leaving both his companion and the party in question.

In the process of doing just that, he bumps into Sue, another work colleague, whom he has secretly always fancied, but could never pluck up the courage to ask out. Sue has a warm welcome for him, inviting him over to join a small group of her friends. He is initially fearful that he will be seen by her and them as being physically anxious, but her warmth, smile and positive engagement begins to win him over. Internally, his mirror neuron and OFC are sensing an immediate empathy bond and exert a calming effect on his amygdala, which begins to settle down. Sue's positive body language as well as her warm and encouraging conversational style are also being picked up by his social brain, with this information being also transferred by his spindle cells to the relevant social structures. His OFC's decision to leave the party is rapidly overturned. Thus begins a relationship that will blossom over the coming months and years. He still has a lot of work to do to manage his social anxiety, but with Sue's assistance he will in time finally develop the necessary skills to deal with it.

If you can relate to Simon's story, hopefully some of the skills explored later in this book will be of assistance to you as well.

Our Language Networks

Before leaving our discussion on the neuroscience of how we emotionally connect, it is important to explore the role of our language networks in the brain. Much of the way in which we socially connect with each other, as discussed, is non-verbal and unconscious. But what defines us most as human beings is our ability to communicate through language, whether through the spoken or written word.

It is the left side of the brain that is key to your ability to both produce and comprehend language. The main area for the production and articulation of language is called Broca's area and it is situated in the left frontal lobe of the brain, above your left eye. It may also play some role in your comprehension of language. If we develop a stroke involving this area, for example, we will be unable to verbalize what we want to say, a condition we call expressive aphasia.

The main area involved in the comprehension and language-processing of speech is called Wernicke's area, and this is situated in the left temporal lobe of the brain over your left ear. Both Broca's and Wernicke's areas are close to one another in the brain and connected by a thick bundle of nerve fibres, so work closely together in practice. It is this language network, which primarily involves the left side of the brain (90 per cent in right-handed people and 70 per cent in left-handed people), which plays such an important role in the way in which we communicate with each other, both in how we verbalize language and how we comprehend just what is being said, both essential parts of emotional connection. As a matter of interest, there are also strong links between this network and our insular cortex, which is so important in your emotional world and self-awareness.

There is also increasing awareness that the tone and pitch of how we speak allows us to convey a wide variety of emotional meaning in what we are saying to one another; and that the language networks probably link with other areas of the brain when it comes to a full comprehension of what we are saying to one another at any one time.

The Neuroscience of Hearing vs Listening

While often conflated, there are some key differences between hearing and listening. *Hearing* involves sound waves, from the outside, passing through your eardrums into your inner ear, where they stimulate thousands of little hair cells, which vibrate. These vibrations are then converted into electric impulses that travel into your auditory cortex. This part of the brain, which is present on both sides and situated over your ears, then translates these impulses into sounds as you know them. Hearing is therefore considered a bottom-up process in the brain. Bottom-up processes involve sensory inputs such as hearing, vision, touch, smell and taste. Clearly, how the brain responds to these inputs will require a top-down processing of such information and this is what happens in real life.

Your brain also has an amazing capacity to filter out unwanted noises, allowing you to focus on information of greatest interest to you. This is important, as otherwise your mind and brain would be swamped by the cacophony of noise emanating from our busy modern world.

Our brains are hard-wired to focus especially on verbal language, particularly if it is a language that we understand, rather than the wide variety of other sounds flowing in from our external environment. This does not mean however that we are actively listening, more that our brain automatically tends to become aware of what others are saying verbally.

Listening on the other hand occurs when you consciously decide to focus attention on what another person is saying to you.

This can be seen as a 'top-down' processing of the information being imparted to you. Where you focus the attention of your PFC on what the person is emotionally and cognitively trying to share with you, filtering out information that you deem unnecessary. This will involve many of the social brain networks previously discussed. We will be discussing the importance of active or empathetic listening in the next chapter.

The major difference between hearing and listening from a brain networking perspective is therefore whether we decide to focus or not to focus our full attention on what a person is saying to us. How often do we hear what someone is saying but fail to truly listen?

The Listening Ear

Mother Nature has given each one of us two ears, one on the right side and one on the left. Common sense would say that both would play an equal role in how we hear and listen to what we as human beings are saying to one another. As with so much of neuroscience, it is not so simple! We are designed so that, in general, the right side of the brain controls the left side of the body and vice versa. The movements of my left arm and left leg for example are controlled by the right side of my brain and vice versa.

But, as already discussed, the main language centres are situated in the left side of the brain. In particular, the main language centre involved in the comprehension of language, Wernicke's area, is situated in the left cortex. The importance of this then is that all the information flowing in from your right ear arrives primarily in the left cortex, which houses Wernicke's area. So your capacity to comprehend language is usually faster and more efficient when using your right ear. This would seemingly give the right ear a major advantage in social situations, and this turns out to be the case in general. This is why, if you are in the middle of a noisy party or occasion and desperately trying to focus on what another person is telling you, you unconsciously tend to tilt your right ear towards the person.

Thankfully the poor old left ear does come into its own when we are trying to focus on the emotional content of what someone is saying, or appreciating the sounds of Mother Nature or listening to music. This occurs because the left ear feeds into the right side of your brain, which, as already discussed, plays a central role in how you process emotions.

This right ear–left ear divide is important in relation to emotional connection. If you want a better understanding and comprehension of the details of a situation when listening, shift your right ear towards the person. If, however, you are interested, as most good emotional connectors are, in the emotional content of what a person is trying to say to you, perhaps tilt the left ear. More on this later.

PART TWO

WEEK 1:

WHAT DID YOU SAY AGAIN?

3. Listening Skills

Is Mother Nature trying to tell us something in providing human beings with two ears but only one mouth? I have always believed that how you listen is more important than what you say. We have even evolved in such a way, as discussed in the last chapter, so that your right ear listens in a slightly different way to the left. This is why we are going to begin this section on verbal skills by exploring the importance of developing good *listening* skills. This might be the most important chapter in this book.

How We Listen

Let's begin our discussion by focusing on 'how' we listen or, to be more precise, how we frequently *don't* listen to each other's everyday conversations. The harsh reality is that most of us are not good listeners, primarily because, like it or not, we are 'self-obsessed', the opposite of what being a good listener should be all about.

How often do you find yourself 'hearing' but not 'listening to' what a person is saying to you? Or, even more tellingly, listening, but only with the express agenda of focusing the attention of the other person on something of particular interest to yourself?

Or perhaps you are someone who only listens if the information coming in fits with 'your narrative' of how life should be? These are three common examples of unhelpful listening routines, which so many of us fall into. Let's explore them further.

Hearing but Not Listening

In this first scenario, someone is speaking to us and while we are theoretically hearing what they are saying, we are not paying attention to it. How often is our mind, for example, off somewhere else, possibly thinking about what we are going to have for dinner, or who will win the match that evening? Every one of us can relate to this situation as it happens constantly throughout our daily working and domestic lives. Why does this happen? The answer is simple: we can only focus our brains and minds on a small amount of information at any one time.

We therefore have a choice when someone is talking to us about something of relevance to them: we may choose to continue hearing but not really listening to what they are saying, just absorbing the bare bones of the discussion; or we focus attention instead on some subject or issue of greater interest to ourselves. We could call this a form of 'passive listening', where we are vaguely listening to, but not really focusing any significant attention on, the essence of the conversation in question. In my experience, this is one of the commonest forms of listening and one that is very detrimental to our goal of becoming a good emotional connector. Let's see how this would play out in real life. Maybe you can see yourself in Tom's interaction with Jim.

Tom's Story

Tom meets a work colleague Jim at the coffee machine. Jim, with a big smile on his face, launches into a discussion of the craic he and some of his buddies had the night before, when out on a pub crawl. Jim is an extrovert who loves people and is never short of a few words. Tom however finds Jim boring and would happily have shut down the conversation, but finds himself trapped at the coffee machine, so internally 'shuts down' and focuses in his head on an assignment he is struggling with at work.

As far as Tom is concerned, he is listening politely to what Jim is saying and simply waiting for the conversation to run out of steam. What he does not realize is that Jim's internal social brain is unconsciously picking up Tom's negative body language and lack of interest, even though Tom seems to be listening to him. As a result, Jim shuts down the conversation and makes his way back to his work station feeling slightly irritated, without really knowing why. Tom, on the other hand, breathes a sigh of relief that this trivial conversation is over and congratulates himself on taking the time to listen to his colleague, despite his unspoken lack of interest. Of even greater import, during the conversation he has discovered an angle on his work problem, which had been his main focus of attention during the whole conversation.

What Tom has missed of course is the possible richness of an interaction with a cheerful extrovert like Jim, who exhibits many characteristics of the simple bumble bee, which moves from flower to flower, all the time gathering nectar, while enriching the natural world in the process, receiving and giving at the same time. Jim too has missed out on a golden opportunity to improve his own listening skills, which leave a lot to be desired. By focusing the conversation only on himself and not truly listening to or showing any interest in his fellow colleague, he finishes the conversation feeling deflated. Both Tom and Jim are perfect examples of hearing but not listening, and they clearly have work to do on their listening skills.

Listening with an Agenda

In this second scenario, you may find yourself listening to another person but, instead of focusing your full attention on what they are saying at the time, you are listening with an agenda, with the express purpose of bringing the conversation as quickly as possible to a subject or topic of greater relevance or interest to you. This is another common form of listening and, once again, each one of us is guilty of doing just that on a daily basis. You may find yourself feeding into your natural human obsession with yourself and what is going on in your own personal world. At other times, however, you may be listening with the agenda of seeking out something you desire from the other person, for example to gain an advantage over a competitor or to encourage them to purchase an item or service from you. These are only some of the common reasons for listening with an agenda. Sometimes you may be consciously listening like this but, most of the time in my experience, you do so unconsciously, not fully grasping how unhelpful this form of listening is in your life. How it can often block your ability to truly network with others.

Let's once again see how this would play out in real life. Maybe you can see yourself in Judy's interaction with Sandra.

Judy's Story

Judy bumps into one of her neighbours, Sandra, at the local supermarket. Sandra begins to open up to her about her difficulties in coping with her mum's advancing dementia. Judy makes all of the right noises of sympathy, but unconsciously slips into only half-listening to what her neighbour is saying as Judy has been hoping to bump into Sandra for some time. This is because Sandra works as a personal assistant to the managing director of a company that Judy has been hopeful of joining.

Judy, having seemingly listened carefully to Sandra and made the right noises about her mother's condition, now thinks that it's time to nudge the conversation towards what is really of interest to her, namely Sandra's relationship with her boss. Instead of truly listening to and empathizing with Sandra about her current situation, Judy attempts to shift the conversation back to Sandra's work situation and her relationship with her boss.

What Judy is missing is that, as with Tom in the previous example, Sandra's internal social brain is picking up unconsciously that her neighbour is only half-listening to her discussion about her mother's illness. As a result, she pulls back from the conversation and gives out very little information on her current working situation. She politely thanks Judy for listening to her woes, but breaks off the conversation, citing being late for an appointment.

Both women leave the encounter feeling slightly irritated, without really understanding why. Judy feels that she has lost an opportunity to get some valuable insights that might have increased her chances of joining Sandra's company (even though in her mind she has 'listened' to the latter's difficulties with her mother's situation). While Sandra on the other hand feels that although Judy has seemingly listened to her story, she has not genuinely connected with her emotionally and feels a little hurt about this. Why would Judy want to know anything about her work situation, when all that matters at present is her difficulties in looking after her mum!

If Judy had instead buried her hidden agenda and listened actively and with empathy to Sandra's story and tried to assist her emotionally or practically, then both women could have really networked. If in the future this inadvertently led to a discussion at a different time about Sandra's workplace and boss, then it would have simply been a by-product of this. This is a classic example of how a lack of emotional connection skills in the form of active listening can damage potential life possibilities.

Listening to Your Own Narrative

The third way in which many of us choose to listen is to do so only if the information coming back to us fits in with our own view of the world, or the narrative that we follow. We only listen to, or hear, what we want to hear. This is once again an unhealthy form of listening, and one that can lead to many misunderstandings.

How often have you been in the middle of a conversation about something of interest or relevance to you, when the listener suddenly changes topic, seemingly midstream? We immediately feel slightly irritated and put out. It can almost seem rude to us at the time. But why would the listener behave in this manner?

The commonest reason for this form of listening is that the person in question is only interested in issues that fall into their view of the world and simply switches off listening to any information or story that does not fit into this narrative. Sometimes, it is simply that the person listening has an extremely limited range of interests and is unable to move outside of this range. But sometimes, and of greater concern, they have developed some fixed, almost irrational views of how the world should be, and will only listen to information that supports and strengthens such views. We will see this in practice in the example below, when Nuala tries to share with one of her husband's friends, Paul, about her son coming out as being gay.

This fixity of thinking can be one of the biggest challenges that one can face when wanting to become a really good listener. For the opposite of fixity is openness, and great networkers who have such listening skills have learned to reshape many of these fixed beliefs, to allow them to truly connect with others.

Nuala's Story

Nuala meets up with a friend of her husband's at a party and both are getting on reasonably well, although she is finding him, in her own words to her partner later, 'heavy weather'. During the conversation, Nuala opens up about how proud they are of their son Jimmy, who has recently come out as being gay, and how he is now in a loving relationship. How supportive the whole family have been of Jimmy's situation and how much they admire his honesty and openness.

Suddenly, she notices that Paul is no longer listening, but looking over her shoulder at someone else. He then abruptly interrupts her flow of conversation and changes the topic to something inane. Shortly afterwards, he excuses himself and she finds herself alone, wondering what she has done.

In practice, Paul is someone with extremely fixed views on many issues and one of these relate to homosexuality. If anything to do with such areas comes up in conversation, he quickly shuts down listening. Only later, when Nuala reveals what has happened to her husband, does he explain that Paul is renowned for only listening if the subject in question is of interest to him, and that he is well known for his views on LBGT+ issues. He is also known for only opening up about such subjects to people who share his views.

For Paul to become a good listener, it is clear that he will have to challenge his narrative or fixed views on the world. It is going to be extremely difficult to either actively listen or become a good networker, otherwise.

Active Listening

If we take the three scenarios above, where there are obvious blocks to becoming a good listener, the first one stands out as being the most common listening error in practice. Most of us are unconsciously switching off from conversations all the time, not for any particular reason, not because we have an agenda or fixed narrative about ourselves and the world, but because we just don't 'pay attention'. For attention is clearly what real listening is actually about. This is sometimes called 'active listening', and this has to be our goal.

Active listening involves focusing in on three key aspects of a conversation. The first one relates to the finer details of what is being said, the second relates to the emotions being expressed by the person in question, and the third to the importance of silence. It also involves being empathetic, but we will be exploring this skill later. In this section we are going to explore these three aspects of active listening in greater detail.

Listening – It's All about the Finer Details

Most of us when listening to a friend, colleague or loved one tend to go for the 'sense' of what they are telling us, rather than focusing on the finer details. This at first glance seems to be eminently sensible. Rather than wasting a lot of precious time and brain power on focusing on and retaining details of a conversation, we tend to summarize the main points mentally and move in quickly to respond to the mental picture created. We have a sense of what the person is trying to communicate and are happy to go along with this.

But as the adage goes, 'the devil is in the detail'. What this means is that the smaller details may be a lot more important than we think at the time. This is especially true when listening to a person who is struggling with some significant issue in their lives, as with Sandra in the earlier example.

We can easily jump to the conclusion, at such times, that we have an overview of the situation and don't require any further details. The reality of course is that unless we focus on and pay attention to these small details, which is often best done with quiet targeted questions, we may be missing out on the reality of the person's situation. In Judy's case, for example, it would be important to listen carefully, and to ask questions, to see how her mother's condition is really impacting on Sandra's everyday life. This would be real active listening. If Judy in the above example had done just that, she would have gained a deeper, more profound understanding of Sandra's current difficulties.

If any of us were to sit down, an hour after a conversation, which may have lasted for up to fifteen minutes, and on a piece of paper write down the details discussed, we would be shocked to discover just how little information relating to the finer details we had retained. Try it and see for yourself. It is quite illuminating! The reality, as already noted, is that we are self-obsessed and only focus on the main details, usually the ones of greatest interest to ourselves. This is not a criticism or an accusation that we are being consciously selfish – rather that we slip into these lazier forms of listening unconsciously and keep repeating them till they become a habit.

Clearly if you can relate to the above and you desire to become a good listener, you will have to develop a different approach, and we will discuss how to do this in the following chapter. It might be useful, for starters, if you are trying to tease out such finer details, to tilt your right ear towards the person in question. This will allow, as detailed in the last chapter, the left side of your brain to focus its full attention on eliciting such details.

Listening – It's All about the Emotions

The second key ingredient to active listening is to become increasingly aware of the importance of the emotions expressed or implied during a conversation. In general we are probably better at sensing or picking up the emotional content of what someone is saying to us than at focusing on the finer details. Despite this, many of us are often insufficiently focused on how the person talking to us is feeling emotionally, both about the topic being discussed, and in general. This can occur because we are, on occasion, self-obsessed about something else going on emotionally or otherwise in our own lives, or are simply not 'tuning in' sufficiently to what the other person is expressing emotionally.

The reality of course is that often the emotional content of a conversation might be of greater import than the actual details of the issue being discussed. The good or active listener is more attuned to picking up on emotions such as anxiety, sadness, depression, hurt, anger or frustration, for example, than a poor listener. This allows them to sensitively ask deeper questions, which might assist the other person to open up and share how they are truly feeling at that moment in time.

I have always believed that this is the deepest form of listening – where we are listening, not just to what the person is saying or not saying but, at a more profound level, to how they feel. Let's suppose you meet a friend, who has just lost a parent to cancer. If you are a good listener, you will not just focus on the details of how the parent died, their funeral and how your friend is coping with the changes in their lives as a result of their death, but you will also check in on how your friend is doing emotionally. You may, with the assistance of a few gentle questions, discover more about what is really going on in their life as a consequence of their loss.

Great listeners are those who realize that clueing in to the emotional aspect, spoken or unspoken, of a conversation is often where they will make the deepest and truest connections. It might be useful here to tilt your left ear towards the person, if trying to tease out the emotions being expressed, as this will allow the right side of your brain to assist you to do just that.

Listening – Sometimes It's about the Silences

The third ingredient to become an active listener is learning how to understand the importance of silence. This might seem paradoxical. How could a period of silence be of assistance to us when listening? Surely listening must involve hearing the spoken word? The reality, of course, is that the good listener can frequently learn more from a period of silence than from anything the person has verbalized during a conversation. Journalists and chat show hosts who stand out in their professions are those who have learned to understand the importance of silence during an interview. Why? The answer is that sometimes silence can allow the other person a period of reflection, a time to gather their thoughts, or indicate that there is something of importance yet to be revealed.

Here are some common situations where silence can play a critical role in how we listen:

1. If someone suddenly becomes silent during a conversation, it may be that they are feeling emotionally moved by the nature of what is being discussed and need some time to regain their composure. By staying silent, you are giving them that time.

2. It may be that there is something really important that they are trying to say and we must give them the time, through respectful silence, to pluck up the courage or to formulate it in their head, before expressing it.

3. There are times when an active listener will sense that there is no reason to fill in the gaps. That both people understand emotionally where the other is at, and words would only get in the way. Silence acts as the filler. In such situations, silence may be more powerful than any words spoken.

4. Sometimes silence can be important for what is 'not' being said by the person in question. If skilled at listening, we will sense that there is important information being withheld from us. A period of silence can be a quiet reminder that you are recognizing this to be the case, while respecting the right of the other person to withhold this information at that moment in time, if not comfortable with revealing it. It is also leaving the door open for a future conversation, if the person changes their mind.

5. Lastly, especially with those we are closest to, silence can be comfortable for both people, as we are listening to each other at a deeper level, where words are unnecessary. There will be many who have had the joy of a long-term relationship who understand this form of listening and the place of silence in it.

Silence is difficult for us all. Nature abhors a vacuum, always wanting to rush in and fill the space. We too, as human beings, are frequently uncomfortable about leaving a period of silence that develops during a conversation unfilled. But if there is anything that over forty years of being a medical doctor has taught me, it is that such periods of silence often reveal more than the longest of conversations.

If you wish to become a good listener therefore, you will have to be comfortable in clueing in to such periods of silence and feel secure enough in yourself to do so. This could be best described as 'listening to the silence', something that few of us are comfortable doing. Another of those listening skills that is so useful to acquire.

Now that we have explored in detail what assists and what hampers us from becoming skilled listeners, let's explore how you can develop and practise your skills in this area, a life-transforming process.

As we detailed in chapter one, you can choose any of the skills in the upcoming section on verbal strategies to include as part of your four-week programme.

4. How to Improve Your Listening Skills

At the heart of improving your listening skills is the concept of 'paying attention', something that all of us struggle with. The buzzword of the moment is 'mindfulness', seen by many as being of great assistance in combating many of our mental health challenges. Yet those who teach mindfulness constantly remind us how difficult it is for us to focus our attention on anything for even a short period of time. It is just the way we humans and our brains have evolved over time. Those who have developed a better understanding of what mindfulness is, and practise it consistently in their lives, notice however how their capacity to focus their attention on something in the present moment begins to improve.

So too with listening skills. It takes time to develop these skills but, with practice, you too will notice that your ability to focus your attention on what others are saying will gradually improve. Eventually this technique will become embedded in your everyday life, with astonishingly positive benefits.

We will be focusing on the following three listening skills:

1. *Skill One* will involve you focusing on the finer details of specific conversations, something that many of us rarely

do. This will allow you to move away from a routine of just 'summing up' quickly in your mind the essence of what someone is saying, and instead take the time to go into the topic in greater depth, if appropriate.

2. *Skill Two* will involve you focusing less on the finer details of specific conversations, and more on the emotional messages being conveyed at a deeper level.

3. *Skill Three* will involve you paying attention to the importance of silence during particular conversations and practising when, where and how to listen and learn from such silences.

You may choose any one of these three skills to be one of the verbal strategy skills included in your four-week programme. I would strongly advise choosing listening skills first before including conversational skills, which we will be covering later in this verbal strategy section.

Analysing How You Listen

Before we get stuck into the skills, it is first important to assess where you are right now. How good a listener are you in practice? Are there areas where you can improve? It can be extremely helpful to analyse your everyday listening skills by answering some of these queries.

We all have our own individual style of listening and maybe you are already a skilled listener and will find this exercise to be unnecessary. For most of us, however, this introductory exercise can be a chastening experience. You must be prepared to accept with humility the likelihood that how you listen to those you encounter at present may leave a lot to be desired. Do not be despondent if this turns out to be the case. Join the majority of the human race, most of whom struggle in this area. This should be seen, rather, as a learning or information-gathering exercise.

Let's therefore begin by spending a few days analysing the quality of your listening techniques at this moment in time, with a special emphasis on the three common listening errors noted in the last chapter. This is an important exercise, as it will focus your attention, probably for the first time in many years, on just how 'you' listen.

Listening Observation Exercise

For the next three days, focus your attention on every conversation you have. Carefully pay attention to whether you are some-one who hears a lot, but rarely listens (a passive listener); someone who regularly listens with your own agenda in mind; someone who only focuses on information that fits your narrative; or someone who quickly jumps to conclusions based on the minimum amount of information you have listened to. You may even notice other idiosyncratic tendencies in listening, separate to what we have discussed.

Each evening in question, take a few moments to write up some insights into what you learned from your observations of how you listened during that particular day. These observations can be quite revealing.

It is important when doing this exercise, as with mindfulness, not to attempt to change at this stage the listening styles you uncover, rather simply pay attention to them. In other words, become more aware of just how 'you' listen in general. The skills that follow will help you to make any changes deemed necessary.

This exercise assists you in several ways to become a good listener.

1. It trains you to begin focusing conscious attention on what up to this point was a largely unconscious pattern of listening.
2. It assists you in gathering accurate information as to the type of listening styles that you routinely apply in your everyday conversations.
3. It allows you to spot unhelpful patterns or habits of listening, which are clearly blocking your goal of becoming a skilled listener.
4. It may also shine a light on how poorly you handle periods of silence, how few fine details you obtain or retain during a conversation and how little you are aware of the emotional nature of what the person is saying to you.

If you faithfully carry out this exercise, by the end of the three days you will have a much clearer picture of your everyday listening style, what you are doing positively or negatively and the areas you clearly need to work on.

You are now ready to work on the critical skills to assist you in becoming an active listener. The development of these skills will involve applying some simple exercises to your everyday life. After reading through these three skills, choose whichever one you feel you need to work on most and make this the focus of your first week in your personalized four-week programme.

Skill One: How to Focus on the Finer Details

As discussed in the previous chapter, many of us glide over the details of routine conversations, tending instead to mentally summarize or jump to conclusions about the essence of what the person is saying to us. This means skimming over superficially, in many situations, the smaller, finer, crucial pieces of information that might shine a totally different light on what the person is really saying to us. If you wish to become a skilled listener it is useful to train yourself to focus on the smaller print, or finer details of conversations. To do so, you will have to improve your capacity to both obtain and retain these elusive pieces of information, which will make all the difference!

At the heart of this exercise is the word 'attention'. To focus on the finer details of a conversation requires initially a 'conscious' effort to pay attention to what the person is saying to you. This will usually require you to ask specific nuanced questions about details that may initially seem unclear to you and to zone in carefully on the replies received.

Listening Skills: Exercise One
For one week, consciously focus on the small details in every conversation, however seemingly irrelevant such minutiae may seem. Listen carefully to exactly what the person is trying to tell you. If you feel you have elucidated the details that matter, then feel happy to reply accordingly. If, as will usually be the case when you are actively listening, you discover that you have not acquired the exact or finer details relating to the subject in question then begin to practise asking gentle, nuanced questions to tease out exactly what information they are trying to share with you. You can only carry out this exercise faithfully if you put aside any agendas

or fixed mindsets while performing it. Otherwise, you are not truly remaining open to what the person is saying, only focusing on what you want to hear, which of course is the opposite of what this exercise is training us to do.

This exercise will often feel quite odd to begin with, as is the case in acquiring any new skills. You may feel quite self-conscious and bothered that the other person will look at you strangely when you ask such questions. To your surprise, however, you will notice that the person is often quite happy to share such finer details with you. They will in fact be appreciative that you are taking the time and effort to genuinely listen to and show interest in their story. Their social brain will also sense this and act accordingly.

You may often notice, having teased out the finer details of a particular situation, that what you discover is subtly different from what you initially assumed it to be. This is because you have used different parts of your brain to focus attention on the true essence of the conversation. Do remember to tilt that right ear towards the person when performing this exercise, to assist you in picking out these nuggets of information.

It might also be useful to write in your diary if there were specific conversations where you felt you had elucidated information that previously might have remained unsaid. What did you learn from performing this exercise that day? Are you finding it increasingly easier to perform? Will it change how you listen from this moment on?

Skill Two: How to Focus on the Emotional Content of a Conversation

As discussed previously, the emotional content of a conversation is often as important as the finer details revealed. Your emotional brain is more powerful than your logical or rational brain. Human beings, therefore, are usually more affected by their emotional reactions to situations or conversation. How often can you recall, for example, being more affected by the emotions emanating from the person you were listening to than the information conveyed during the conversation?

Sometimes, however, we may not be clueing in as much as we should to the emotions conveyed in a conversation, and miss out on so much as a result. This often happens when we ourselves are either preoccupied with other issues of relevance in our lives, or simply not switched on enough to pick up the emotional vibrations emanating from the person in question. It is also key that, when we do sense the emotions being expressed, we validate these emotions. We will be discussing this in greater detail when dealing later with empathy. In this section, we will focus simply on picking up the emotions in the first place.

It is important to try to improve your skill in this area. To do so, I suggest the following exercise. It might be useful to tilt the left ear more towards the person when carrying this one out, to allow the right side of your brain the chance to focus on the emotions being expressed.

Listening Skills: Exercise Two

For one week, consciously concentrate during every conversation you have, no matter how trivial or seemingly irrelevant, on the emotions being expressed by the person you are listening to. This involves doing the opposite of what you have done in the previous exercise, where you were focusing on the finer details. In this exercise, I want you to simply ask yourself – how is the person feeling emotionally as they relate their story? Do they seem happy, sad, hurt, angry, frustrated and so on?

If unsure as to how they are feeling emotionally about this situation, don't be afraid to ask some gentle, nuanced questions that might shed more light on the subject. Suppose you feel they are pleased or happy, but are not fully sure, you might ask an open-ended question such as 'Am I picking up some vibes that you are pleased with this situation?' Or you may feel they are frustrated by something but confirm this, with something like 'This seems to be really getting to you?' This allows the person to share with you whether this is the case or not. Don't leave the conversation till you feel comfortable that you have a good sense of where the person is at emotionally.

You might also sense on other occasions, if actively listening, that the person is struggling emotionally in some other area, separate from the one being discussed. A good example of this might be where you sense the person seems sad or depressed. A good observation/implied question here might be 'You don't seem to be yourself today, you seem a little down in yourself, from the last time we chatted.' This allows the person to fill in, or not, further details as to how they are feeling emotionally, at that moment in time.

This is real listening and, when done with gentleness and empathy, can reveal much more than the simple details of what is going on in a person's life. You are also implying that you are genuinely listening to how they are, and that you are there for them, if help is needed. The real skills of an effective emotional connector.

When listening emotionally, you will also, often unconsciously, be focusing not just on the emotions being expressed verbally but also on their body language cues. These will often, as will be discussed in future chapters, tip us off as to just how a person is really feeling about a situation during such a conversation. If you are picking up something in this manner, it becomes easier to tease out with some questions why this might be the case. More on this later.

This exercise is a powerful one as it teaches us how listening emotionally allows us to connect at a deeper level, and often at a faster speed, than relying on the details of what someone is sharing with us. It is the shortcut to becoming a good listener. If observant, you will also notice where you have connected emotionally in this manner, how you have created a newer, deeper bond with the person you are listening to.

Write down in your diary, if you feel it is of assistance to you, details of any conversations that affected you or the other person emotionally, and if so why. Are you noticing that you are becoming increasingly adept at picking up how the person is feeling emotionally? Are your interactions becoming more fulfilling? Are you networking better with others as a result? As the week progresses, the answer to all of these should be 'yes'. If not, then try and analyse what you might be doing wrong. Are you still focusing more on how you feel, rather than how the other person is feeling? Are you still focusing more on the details, and less on the emotions being expressed? In this way, you will quickly become increasingly skilled in this area.

Skill Three: How to Focus on the Importance of Silence

In the previous chapter, we explored the many faces of silence and why they are so important to how we listen. It's my belief that managing silence is one of the most underrated elements of becoming a good listener. Learning to cope with and create silence has been purposefully left to the last of the three skills as it is, in my opinion, the most challenging one to learn and practise. It is perhaps the highest form of communication, which seems strange. That we can learn more from a vacuum than by filling it! But if you persevere, this skill will bear much fruit.

If you find yourself struggling with either managing a period of silence that develops during a conversation, or uncomfortable with creating such a vacuum if appropriate, the following exercise may be of great assistance.

Listening Skills: Exercise Three

For one week, consciously focus on any periods of silence that develop during routine conversations that ensue in your normal everyday life. Your first task will be to sit on your natural tendency to fill conversational vacuums that occur. Instead, let the period of silence develop and see where it brings the conversation to. This will be a difficult task, yet one that may prove to be most enlightening, as you learn to understand the value of silence.

Focus especially on what the period of silence means to the person you are listening to. Do they become extremely uncomfortable? Does it allow them an opportunity to put their thoughts in order, or reveal something of great emotional importance? Do they perhaps choose, following an internal struggle, not to reveal information that both of you sense is important? Or do they simply wish to bring the conversation naturally to a conclusion, anxious to complete some other task? It can be really interesting to write in your diary what you learn about such silences.

When you have become comfortable with listening during such times of silence, consciously practise, during this week, allowing a period of silence to grow and develop during routine conversations (if deemed appropriate). In the beginning you may feel extremely uncomfortable allowing this, but after a while you will find it easier to let such silences develop. You may sense, for example, that the person wants to say something of importance to you, but is awaiting a gap in the conversation to reveal it. It may be that you are sensing something of emotional import to the other person and allow the silence to occur, to allow them to ventilate it. It could be that you sense that the person is uncomfortable in discussing a particular matter and by allowing the silence to grow, you are allowing them an opportunity to change the topic. This of course means that you are actively listening to them at a deeper level and not focusing on your own agenda.

Once again, you might find it useful to write down in your diary what you have learned from creating such silences. Have they taught you anything? Have you learned some valuable information, which you otherwise might have overlooked or missed out on completely? Did you feel it was a useful tool to add to your listening skills?

Let's now see how Maria learned to put all of the above skills into action. Maybe you might see elements of yourself in her story.

Maria's Story

Maria loves to talk, a trait present from childhood. She has, however, always struggled with listening. In her mind, she doesn't feel this to be the case. Maria genuinely believes that she spends much of her time listening to friends and family. In practice, however, she is a superficial listener, rapidly jumping to what she believes to be the essence of a conversation and then verbally elaborating on what she thinks the person she is listening to should do. She has a great heart, but unfortunately regularly misses out on both the finer details and emotions being expressed by others. As for silence, this is a foreign country. Maria would never let a silence develop, rapidly rushing in to fill the vacuum.

Her world comes grinding to a halt, however, when her boyfriend Pete decides to break off their relationship, saying that, although he is fond of her, Maria is too self-obsessed and never really listens to him. Maria is shocked by his comments and shares them with her best friend Jenifer, who gently informs her that there may be some truth in what Pete is alleging. While Maria is a lovely person and a dear friend, she does have some issues in terms of her listening skills and would perhaps benefit from working on them. Pete is just one relationship that has not worked out, but active listening skills might turn out to be of relevance in every part of her life, not just in her personal relationships.

Maria chooses to take on board Jenifer's advice and with the assistance of a life coach, Martin, begins to work on her listening skills. Martin suggests that they begin by Maria consciously observing her listening style for three days. She begins to notice quite rapidly how she is hearing what others are saying, but not actively listening in any meaningful way. How she focuses on issues of importance in her own life, rather than on what others are saying to her. It is a chastening experience and Maria has to do a lot of soul searching as a consequence!

Martin then suggests she spend a week focusing during conversations on the finer details of what others are saying to her. She finds this extremely challenging. Her instinctive tendency is to acquire a fast global picture of what the person is saying and seek to jump in with some comments or advice. She forces herself however to focus intently on the actual details. To actively listen more and say a lot less. Within days she becomes more adept at asking the nuanced questions if she senses that the details need fleshing out. The results are quite revealing. She finds herself bonding more intimately with others during such conversations as they respond positively to her interest and reveal information that would otherwise have remained hidden. In the process, she discovers that there is a great richness in the finer details uncovered.

With Martin's assistance she then spends a second week focusing on the emotional content of what others are trying to convey to her. Martin explains that this is a shortcut to becoming a good listener. Maria once again finds this task challenging but very rewarding, as it opens up a new world to her, namely that of emotions. Once again, it requires extreme focus and concentration during conversations to focus on the other person's emotional state. Over a short period of time, however, she becomes increasingly comfortable in her ability to sense where the other person is at emotionally.

As a result of performing this exercise, Maria is forced to admit to Martin that this is why she has lost Pete, as she had previously been extremely poor at sensing where people were at emotionally during conversations. They agree that applying this skill to future relationships might prove to be a game-changer.

Finally, Maria spends a week embracing the world of silence and learning how to allow it to develop during conversations. How to listen carefully to what the silence was revealing to her and to practise the creation of silences during conversations. She is now able to also retrospectively identify how such silences between Pete and herself, which should have been potential growth opportunities for both, had been rapidly filled by herself, denying these possibilities.

Over the following month, Maria continues to work on her listening skills, and finds the effects to be life-transforming. It might not have saved her relationship with Pete, as it was probably too late to do so. But perhaps future relationships might prove to be deeper and more meaningful for both her and potential partners.

By the end of this period she has also learned the art of putting the listening skills developed into practice, in every facet of her social, personal and working relationships. The change in both her as a person, and in the depth of her interpersonal interactions, is profound. She becomes a deeper, warmer, more connected human being, who now listens much more than she converses. A real emotional connector.

How many of us can see ourselves in Maria's story, where we love to talk but struggle to listen? As a consequence, we may be missing out on the rich tapestry of life and all that it can bring us. For listening is perhaps the greatest communication skill of them all. I cannot recommend highly enough the power of these simple skills in assisting you to become a great listener, and how this in turn will form the bedrock of what it means to be an effective emotional connector. Try them and see!

5. Conversational Skills

In previous chapters, we focused on how you listen. In this chapter, we are going to explore the importance of what comes out of your mouth, in the guise of your everyday conversations. Once again there is much to learn in this area. I have always rated the importance of what we say as being less than our capacity to become a skilled listener. Nevertheless, speech is still the primary means by which we communicate with each other, and conversation the principal vehicle we use for this task, so becoming skilled in this area is next on our agenda.

Most of us believe we are good conversationalists. We in Ireland pride ourselves on having the 'gift of the gab' (in other words that we are expert 'talkers'!). But as with listening, there are common pitfalls, which can prevent us from becoming good conversationalists. Perhaps you recognize yourself in some of them:

- We focus only on ourselves when speaking to others, often failing to recognize that we are doing so
- We only talk about inane matters, avoiding dealing with deeper, more complex areas of life

- Or we do the exact opposite, only interested in conversations dealing with something serious or important in our eyes, what we consider 'weighty matters'
- We struggle perhaps, as do many with social anxiety, to find topics to discuss that we believe others will find interesting
- We block out having a discussion where emotions might be centre stage, uncomfortable in dealing with them
- We like to gossip about others, especially if the gossip is salacious or malicious
- We fail to understand that there are times where not speaking, or remaining silent, might be the most important form of conversation at that particular moment in time
- Or perhaps, we struggle to introduce the important concept of curiosity into conversations.

I am sure that many of us can relate to some of these common pitfalls. Let's explore them in greater detail.

Making Ourselves the Centre of Every Conversation

This is the most common, almost universal, pitfall that we tend to fall into. We simply love to talk about ourselves and can discuss the topic with others endlessly. Let's face it, are we not the most important and interesting person around and the only one worth talking about!! If we are good-humoured about ourselves (which we should always try to be), most of us can relate to the above. It goes back to the core principle, that most of us are self-obsessed. We exist in the centre of our own universe, the star around which all the planets must clearly orbit.

But why should this be an issue and why is it so damaging to our goal of becoming a skilled conversationalist? The answer lies in your brain's capacity to only focus on a small amount of information at any one time. If you are directing its attention during a conversation onto yourself and everything to do with your own world, it is almost impossible to simultaneously focus your attention on what is going on in the world of the person with whom you are conversing. This may lead to them feeling less connected to you. There is also a risk that the conversation you are having together may be of less interest to them, even boring. They may end up on occasion switching off mentally from the conversation, simply nodding politely, while wondering how quickly they can exit.

A second way in which you can inadvertently make conversations all about yourself is to always steer them towards weighty topics that you feel more comfortable discussing and which will, in your mind, showcase you as being more intelligent or knowledgeable. You may not even realize how often you are doing this in everyday meetings and chats, or how boring so many people find such conversations. While you may find the topic in question of great interest to you, they might not. People may also begin to feel lesser, as not as up to speed on the subject as yourself, so mentally pull back.

Perhaps you can relate to this and wonder why people at times seemingly avoid chatting to you. The reason might be that when conversing with you, they feel either uncomfortable or bored and are often seeking a fast exit from the conversation. Clearly, if you can relate to this pattern, it is time to update your conversational skills.

Avoiding Emotional Conversations

As we saw with listening, emotions form a central plank of good conversation. Human beings live and breathe in the world of emotions. They control much of what happens to us in our lives, even if we often fail to notice this. Some of us are, however, uncomfortable with emotions and with any conversation that might dredge them up. This is especially the case if dealing with emotions such as sadness, anxiety, depression or hurt. It is easier for many of us to keep conversations light, even mundane and divert them away from anything that might trigger such emotions.

Good communicators, however, understand the critical role of emotions in conversation. How engaging with another person emotionally is often the shortcut to making a real connection with them. They teach themselves to become comfortable discussing topics with strong emotional content and allowing others in conversation to do the same.

If you notice that you struggle with dealing with emotions that may emerge during a conversation, or can only cope with ones which are more superficial, perhaps it is time to work on your skills in this area.

Gossiping

Apart from discussing the topic of ourselves, human beings from the dawn of time have always loved to gossip about each other. Just look at the popularity of TV soaps or series about the comings and goings of people in their local communities. Whether discussing who is going out with whom, who is having an affair with whom, or who is due to have a baby, the list is endless. The more salacious the information, the better. Gossip, in the majority of cases, can be regarded as a useful means of disseminating information about members of a community for the benefit of all. In real life, most gossip is harmless and can form an integral part of everyday conversations. To this extent it can be seen as carrying out an important social function.

In some situations, however, gossip may be particularly malicious and socially damaging. Thankfully these interactions are actually a lot less common than generally assumed. Still, when they do occur, they are damaging both the person being discussed and the gossiper themselves.

Maybe you too find yourself falling into the pitfall of allowing nastier or malicious gossip to become an integral part of your conversations. If this is the case, it is not only damaging the person about whom you are gossiping, but also reducing your chances of becoming a genuine emotional connector. Those who are skilled in this area understand the importance of showing care and respect for others, if they wish to be seen as genuine and compassionate – critical personal skills we will be visiting later in the book. If you see yourself as someone who tends to engage in such destructive conversations, once again it might be time to review matters.

Ignoring the Role of Silence

When exploring listening, we discussed the importance of silence, and a similar case can be made for its role in conversation. There will be occasions where silence may play a significant role when having a conversation with someone. If meeting someone who has recently lost a loved one, for example, words may simply not cut it. A hug and a moment of reflective silence may be a more powerful form of conversation than any verbalized words, and mean a lot more to the grieving person. It is also so easy for us to chatter away during routine conversations. Most of the time this is both normal and acceptable, as long as you are not monopolizing the conversation, as already discussed. There will be times, however, where you should feel comfortable in remaining silent, not rushing in to fill the vacuum with words, allowing the other person to verbalize what may be really bothering them. This is a real skill, the ability to recognize such periods and feel comfortable in sitting them out, without words getting in the way.

There will be other occasions where you may use silence to get a point across. You may have said something emotional that you feel the person needed to hear, and to consolidate its importance, by remaining silent, you allow them time and space to respond. Great communicators become skilled at using silence in this manner.

Curiosity and Wonder vs Being Bored

It might seem strange to mention the importance of curiosity and wonder when discussing the world of conversation. Yet, I have always believed that when we lose both, our conversations suffer greatly. Children are wonderful in their natural capacity to be in the moment, to be curious about everything they see, to wonder at the simplest of things they come across. How they, in their conversations, often ask the simplest, yet most profound of questions, emanating from this innate sense of curiosity and wonder.

Sadly, many of us as adults lose this natural sense of curiosity about each other and the world around us. This is often evident in how we converse with one another. Instead of considering every human interaction and conversation as an opportunity to learn more about other people and their lives, jobs and hobbies, and discover more about the bits and pieces that make up our existence, we focus on only those parts of interest to ourselves. This is tragic, as we begin to shut down, losing that sense of wonder and curiosity which can make us more rounded, fulfilled human beings. Clearly, if you see yourself here, there is work to be done!

This lack of curiosity is also linked to the common belief that many people suffering from social anxiety have, which is that they are boring. That they cannot come up with subjects that others, in their mind, will find interesting. Others, while not suffering from social anxiety, may also believe that they are boring, and that other people will simply not enjoy being around them. Still others may find particular people boring, without fully understanding why. At the heart of all of these difficulties is a clear misunderstanding that people, rather than the topic of a conversation, can be described as boring. In reality, most people whom we describe as 'boring' are usually only interested in conversing about subjects or topics that we, the listener, find boring. Since the only subjects we, the listeners, find truly interesting are ourselves or issues we are interested in, it is inevitable that we tend to call such people boring. In practice then, it is the topic of conversation that is boring and not them. This insight is a critical one, for if you can grasp it, then developing your conversation skills becomes much simpler.

The same insight applies if you believe that you are boring. It is not you who is boring (we will discuss this error later in the book), rather it is the topic of conversation that you may be having with a person that they might find boring. And once again, since the only topics of conversation they find interesting are themselves and their interests, they may find any other topic brought up by you boring.

If, however, we introduce the concepts of curiosity and wonder into discussions by facilitating others to discuss their lives and interests with us and revelling in the information gained, matters would quickly change. They would now describe you as interesting and not boring, without realizing that you have simply allowed them to converse about themselves.

So too, if you begin to see others as a potential mine of new information about life and the world around us, you will cease to see others as boring. The message is clear. If you wish to become a great conversationalist and networker, you must learn to remove yourself from the centre of conversations and cease believing that you or others can be described as boring.

The Party Story

Let's have some fun now and wander around a work party, observing and eavesdropping on a number of different conversations that are happening to discover just how some of the above conversational difficulties play out in practice.

Seamus is having an animated conversation with **Jenny**, even though she has barely got a word in since it began. Seamus simply loves to hear the sound of his own voice and regularly holds forth on whatever topic he is into, at that moment in time. In this conversation, he is overpowering Jenny, with his views on the current political situation in the country. She is nodding politely, not wanting to hurt his feelings, but privately loathes the whole world of politics, which she finds intensely boring. She has already switched off internally, focusing her energies instead on coming up with an angle that would allow her to end the conversation gracefully to go in search of a friend to talk to.

Meanwhile, **Sally**, who loves gossip, the more salacious the better, is dropping her voice, while in conversation with one of her colleagues, **Joan**, as she reveals that their section head is having an affair. Joan is finding the conversation is making her feel very uncomfortable, as she knows the colleague in question and is aware that his personal relationship has been in difficulties for some time. She finds herself squirming with embarrassment, as Sally delves into the juicier details. She decides to quickly exit the conversation, leaving Sally confused as to what she has done wrong.

In another corner of the room, **Michael**, who suffers from significant social anxiety, goes into a panic when one of his female colleagues, **Charlotte**, joins him for a chat. He has been hanging around at the edge of the group, embarrassed that someone might notice him. He has always been interested in Charlotte, but believes he is not interesting enough for her to take any notice of him. He is frantically searching his mind for some topic to bring up in conversation that she might find interesting, but his mind just goes blank and his anxiety levels skyrocket. Thankfully, Charlotte senses that Michael is shy, but finds him a lot more interesting than many of her other colleagues, who are constantly trying to impress her with the full extent of their knowledge. She gently begins to chat away about the party and how noisy she is finding it, and Michael begins to calm down. Slowly but surely, a real conversation takes shape. Charlotte is very taken by how Michael listens carefully to whatever she says and how he validates her emotionally, as she does him. She also enjoys his quiet sense of humour. She later describes Michael to one of her close friends as being 'so interesting', someone she would like to get to know better.

At the same time **Justin** is really putting his foot in it. He encounters **Caroline**, who lost her dad to a heart attack three months previously and is in the grieving process. He begins by sympathizing with her on her loss, but then comments that she must be happy that her dad is now hopefully in a better place. Caroline goes very quiet as she is deeply upset with this off-the-cuff remark. Justin, instead of reading the silence, misinterprets it as a sign that Caroline does not wish to discuss her dad's death any further, so chases in to fill the vacuum. He switches the conversation to inquire about how she is getting on in relation to her current role in the company. It is inevitable that due to Justin's inability to read the signs, Caroline will exit the conversation as quickly as possible. In fact, she subsequently excuses herself to go to the bathroom, where she breaks down in tears, upset at how little empathy Justin has demonstrated in response to her dad's death.

Bart, in another section of the room, quickly manages to bore his colleague **Damien** to bits, as is his wont, dominating the conversation by focusing on the intricacies of his golf swing. Bart is a low handicapper and loves to let everyone who meets him know how skilled he is at the game. Five minutes later Damien, who has mentally left the conversation shortly after it began, manages to escape by clapping Bart on the shoulder, explaining that he has just spotted a girl he is interested in meeting up with, and doing a runner. Bart is falling into the deep hole of trying to dominate conversations by demonstrating just how expert he is in some aspect of life. Nothing switches the listener off as quickly!

Clearly there will be many other healthier, routine conversations going on at the same party. What the above demonstrates, however, is how often those who believe that they are good conversationalists or social connectors lack real skills in this area. Few of us in general pay much attention to our conversation styles or patterns, often assuming that we are expert in the area, while this may not be the case in practice. It is important to note that none of those at the party who were messing up in this area were deliberately or consciously doing so. It is more that over the years they have fallen into unhelpful patterns or styles of conversing, which have now become quite fixed.

If you can relate to the above, it is important to realize that you are not doomed to remaining like this for life. You can, as we will demonstrate later, develop new healthier conversational skills that can transform your ability to emotionally network.

Now that we have explored the common pitfalls of being an effective conversationalist, it's worth looking at other areas of our personalities and related areas that impact how effective we are in a conversation. These range from the tone we use to who we are talking to, as well as inward-looking factors, such as whether or not we are an introvert or extrovert. Let's start there.

Extroverts vs Introverts

Identifying where you fall on the spectrum of extrovert to introvert has important connotations for your conversational style and emotional connection techniques.

From a personality perspective, many of us classify ourselves as being extroverted, introverted or perhaps as lying somewhere in the middle of these two types. These two traits are increasingly seen as two ends of a continuum. There is much debate on what per cent of the population belong to one or other category. The general view is that around a third of us veer more towards being an introvert, with the rest of us being extrovert or, if someone who can relate to both of these personality traits at different times, classified as being an 'ambivert'.

Are You an Introvert?
If you believe that you are an introvert, you are probably some-one who tends to focus more on your inner thoughts and feelings

and is less dependent on external stimulation. You may tend to be quieter, enjoy spending time in your own company, expend energy quickly when involved in social situations with larger numbers, and feel a real need to recharge your batteries with some quiet time afterwards. You may find it harder to either see the point of, or engage with, routine conversations other than with those whom you feel are important to you. You may say less in social conversations, which may make others incorrectly assume you are uninterested in the discussion or are aloof.

You may feel especially drained after a lot of social interaction, unless with close friends. It does not mean that you do not enjoy socializing, in fact sometimes you may revel in it, but simply find the process quite exhausting. You are in general extremely comfortable being with yourself, and usually quite self-aware. You may have fewer close friends but establish deeper relationships with them. Contrary to opinion, you are not shy, aloof, or socially anxious, you simply do not draw energy from others.

There are some positives of being an introvert from an emotional networking perspective in relation to your conversational skills. You are more likely to have deeper, more emotionally nuanced conversations when you do engage with others, and be comfortable dealing with any period of silence that may develop – both skills that are crucial for effective communication.

Are You an Extrovert?

If an extrovert, you are most likely to be someone who enjoys being with, and actually gains energy from, socializing with other people. You probably love social gatherings, the bigger the better, and are often at your best, for example, when the party is rocking. You will usually tend to be more dominant in conversations, enjoy being the centre of attention and be rarely 'lost for words'. You may be seen as more open, approachable and friendly by others and will probably have a wider group of close friends, but perhaps such friendships are not as deep as those of the introvert.

There are some positives in being an extrovert in relation to your conversational skills. You will usually be quite comfortable with this medium and generally open and interested in people and their lives. You will often be liked by others as a result. You will also be comfortable working as part of a team and in media, PR and marketing occupations because of these strengths. On the negative side, however, you may sometimes fall into the pitfalls described above, such as making yourself the centre of attention during a conversation, overlooking critical silences or not picking up on some emotions being expressed.

It is useful to do some self-analysis on this subject, as it can point us to the areas where you may have to do some work on improving your conversational skills.

If you clearly identify with being an introvert or extrovert, try to keep your natural tendencies from these personality types in mind as you examine your own emotional communication skills. If you're struggling to identify with one or the other, some self-analysis through easily accessible online quizzes can help you figure out where on the introvert–extrovert spectrum you might be.

The Importance of Inconsequential Conversations

One of the arts of conversation is to be able to switch with ease from serious topics on some occasions to seemingly inconsequential chats in others. The importance of the latter cannot be overestimated. Life is difficult for many of us, filled with stressors of every type. It is essential therefore in our everyday lives and conversations to regularly move away from matters or topics that weigh heavily on our minds, to chat away about the most humorous or banal of topics with people we meet. This is an escape valve for the brain and body, allowing us space and time during such conversations, to take our foot off the pedal, de-stress or simply have a bit of fun.

You may fall into the trap of assuming that such conversations are a waste of your valuable time, are beneath you, or that those who engage in such conversations are boring. Maybe if this is the case, it is time for you to have a rethink. Sometimes, having such a conversation with someone at a particular moment in time might bring both parties closer together, creating a future bond. Perhaps at a later stage, this might in turn facilitate a deeper conversation about something of greater relevance, as a bond has now been formed.

The real art, of course, is being able to consciously recognize when it is time to have that seemingly inconsequential conversation and equally when it is time to move into deeper waters, and to be comfortable with both scenarios. Those who achieve this balance will become great networkers.

It's Not What You Say, It's the Way You Say It

What we often fail to recognize is that much of what is expressed during a conversation is influenced by the manner in which it is said. This is regarded as a non-verbal form of communication, known as paralanguage, which deals with how we can transfer information during a conversation, through our tone of voice, pitch, intensity, speech rate and multiple other non-verbal vocal cues. Although technically a non-verbal form of communication, which we will be discussing in the next part of this book, I have chosen to include this particular concept here, in our discussion on conversational skills.

You can change the meaning or intent of the words spoken during a conversation by simply changing one of these vocal non-verbal cues. You may believe, for example, that raising the level of your voice will have a greater effect on the other person, whereas, in my experience, information passed in a quiet, gentle tone often carries a greater impact. You may compliment someone verbally, but the tone of your voice may suggest that you have doubts as to whether such compliments are deserved. You may want to really impress someone in a conversation with information, so speed up your word flow, not recognizing that you are having the opposite effect. You may say something in a tone of voice that sounds cutting or sarcastic. In other situations, you may be trying to convey an important message, but speak so slowly that the other person unconsciously feels denigrated or lesser and, as a result, switches off.

So much of this communication is being done unconsciously, which is what makes this area so difficult for us to grasp. Yet skilled networkers quickly learn to be consciously more aware not only of what they are trying to communicate verbally, but how they are non-verbally getting such messages across. Lack of skills in this area will often prevent you from getting a key message across, as you have conveyed a different non-verbal meaning through the above vocal cues.

What Attributes Will You Need to Become a Skilled Conversationalist?

With all of the above information in mind it is now useful to summarize what attributes you must acquire to become a good conversationalist.

1. **The most important attribute to attain, above all others, is to become an active or skilled listener.** It seems paradoxical, but it is our ability to focus on listening to the details and emotions being expressed by the person we are conversing with that will form the foundation for becoming a talented conversationalist. The poor listener is usually a poor conversationalist or emotional connector.

2. **You must learn how to avoid your natural tendency to focus on yourself**, while conversing with others, or on what is of interest to you in your life. Learn instead how to focus on what the person you are chatting to is saying, even if you do not find this topic to be of particular interest to yourself.

3. **Develop a genuine sense of curiosity about people and their lives.** This does not come easy for many of us, as we love to focus on ourselves and our own lives. If, however, you are prepared to put some effort in here, you will rapidly become a deeper, more rounded, interesting person to talk to, and someone towards whom others will quickly gravitate in social situations, making you of course a skilled emotional networker.

4. **You will have discovered the rich possibilities that silence can bring.** We have discussed earlier its importance in listening. If you can also learn how to use silence as a

tool in certain conversations, you will often learn far more than if you keep talking in the hope that you can elicit further information about something of relevance to the other person.

Now let's explore how you can improve your conversational skills.

6. How to Improve Your Conversational Skills

In the previous chapter we analysed what attributes make for a skilled conversationalist and common pitfalls that many of us fall into in the course of routine daily conversations. Even if you believe that you are adept in this area, there is still room to improve your conversational skills. It doesn't take a huge amount of effort to develop and practise them further. The positive benefits that can accrue from doing so can be truly life-enhancing.

Before you explore the key conversational skills that you may require and how to attain them, let's firstly analyse your individual conversational style.

Analysing How You Converse

Each one of us has our own unique conversational style. Maybe you are already comfortable with your skills in this area. If so, the following exercise will simply assess how effective your skills are and perhaps show up areas where you could improve. For most of us however this exercise can once again be chastening. It is wise to perform it, therefore, with a keen sense of humour. Don't be too hard on yourself if you discover just how much you may be either dominating conversations, focusing too much on what interests you, or failing to let the other person get a word in edgewise. The last is such a common trait.

This exercise is not aimed at pointing out some faults that you may have. Rather, it is an information-gathering exercise, to pinpoint areas where you could improve your conversational skills and hopefully have a bit of fun with yourself in the process.

Conversational Observational Exercise

For the next three days, consciously focus your attention on every conversation you have. I want you to carefully pay attention to what you are doing during such conversations. As with mindfulness, I do not want you to change anything you would normally do during this exercise. This is more of an observational exercise. Ask yourself some of these questions:

- Do you like to talk about yourself most of the time?
- Do you steer the conversation towards areas of interest to yourself?
- Do you ever focus on what the other person is interested in?
- Does your mind wander away if they do begin to steer the conversation their way?
- Do you ever feel curious about a topic they are interested in discussing, or even in the person themselves?
- Do you take yourself too seriously during conversations?
- Do you shut down any emotional interactions during such conversations?
- Does it turn out that your conversational skills are quite adequate? If so, are there any areas that might still need to be worked upon?

Each evening take a few moments to write up some insights into what you learned from your observations of how you conversed during that particular day. These observations can be quite revealing.

If you faithfully carry out this exercise, by the end of the third day you will have a much clearer picture of your everyday conversational style, what you are doing positively and what you clearly need to work on.

Skill One: How to Remove Yourself from Being the Centre of Conversations

This skill will involve you spending time, during conversations, on actively focusing on removing yourself from being at the centre of conversations with others. With the exercise that follows, you will be drilling deeper into the core of what makes a good conversationalist – the ability to focus on others, rather than ourselves. As discussed already, most of us tend to focus only on conversational topics of interest to ourselves and place ourselves at the centre of such interactions. The following exercise is aimed at reversing this tendency.

Conversational Skills: Exercise One

For one week, consciously focus your attention on every conversation that takes place between you and loved ones, colleagues or people you interact with in any area of life. This exercise will involve you actively focusing 'only' on what the other person is saying to you during the conversation. Whatever the topic or information they are sharing with you, it now becomes your sole area of interest. This of course will inevitably require you to remove yourself from being the centre of the conversation.

While this might seem easy, in practice this can be an extremely difficult task to perform. You will notice how you will have to consciously sit on your natural tendency to sweep in and turn the conversation towards an area of interest to yourself. On other occasions you may have to consciously prevent yourself from taking over the conversation to inform the other person what you believe they should do. This exercise becomes especially challenging if you find the topic or subject being discussed extremely boring or uninteresting.

In the beginning you may find yourself really struggling, but persevere and you will find that, bit by bit, you become more adept at focusing on what the other person is saying. Removing yourself from the equation then becomes an easier task to perform.

This is a training exercise. If you carry it out faithfully, by the end of the week you will have laid the foundations for becoming a good conversationalist for life. It is all about 'them' and less about 'me' will become your new maxim. Over time, this skill will become embedded in your social brain and you will find yourself performing it unconsciously.

Once again, it might be useful to write in your diary if there were specific conversations where you found it difficult to achieve your objective. These might be some useful questions to consider:

- Why do you think that is the case?
- Did you find yourself constantly falling back into the pattern of taking over conversation?
- Were there specific topics you found especially boring; if so why?
- What can you do, going forward, to improve your skills in this area?
- What have you learned from the exercise so far?

Skill Two: How to Actively Show Interest

In the next portion of the book, we will be exploring in greater detail non-verbal techniques for showing active interest in the person you are speaking with. In the section above we've looked at how the way we think is crucial for removing ourselves from the centre of the conversation. In this section, we'll look at the importance of body language in relation to how you emotionally connect.

Body language is especially useful for showing interest, but it also has broader importance for conversational skills in general. How often, for example, have you been engaged in conversation with someone who seems distracted, perhaps constantly checking their phone while talking to you, looking into the distance, or found yourself intercepting that dreaded politician-like stare over your shoulder aimed at someone else, deemed to be of greater importance than you? If you're being honest, it can feel disrespectful, even slightly hurtful on occasions, when you encounter such behaviours.

As we discussed in the chapter on neuroscience, the social brain is highly adept at picking up such negative signals, suggesting, sometimes unconsciously, that you quickly cease such conversations and remove yourself from the vicinity or person in question. While you might believe that you are asking the right questions of the person, or focusing on areas of interest to them, none of this will matter if you are not actively showing genuine interest in their conversation. The way we do this of course is by consciously ensuring that our body language is in harmony with our words. This is the basis of this next exercise.

Conversational Skills: Exercise Two

For one week, consciously focus your attention during every conversation, not only on the details of what the other person is saying to you, but also on your body language while conversing with them. This will mean maintaining eye-to-eye contact, consciously tilting your face and body towards them, clearly being in the moment with them, and showing as much intense interest in what they are saying as you can muster at that moment. You must make that person feel as if they are the most important person in your world at that moment in time, not only through your words, but also through your non-verbal cues.

Once again, this can be a remarkably difficult task to perform, as it takes a lot of conscious time, effort and commitment to carry it out. The rewards however are great. You will notice how the person seems to warm towards you, sensing and grateful that you are genuinely taking the time to have a real conversation with them.

In the beginning this will seem very strange, almost artificial in nature. This is because, as we will discuss later, so much of our normal body language is unconscious, so we rarely focus attention on it. After a few days, however, if you practise this exercise during each interaction it will become natural to focus, with attention, on the other person as you both converse. Eventually, it will become second nature for you to do so, adding yet another building block in your quest to becoming a good communicator.

Skill Three: How to Develop Your Sense of Curiosity

This might not seem like an 'obvious' skill to hone; however, I cannot repeat often enough how important it is to truly develop your sense of curiosity about others and life, if you wish to become a talented conversationalist. Over time, if observant, you should notice how much you can learn from others, if willing to open up your mind to focus on any topic of conversation that they may bring up with you.

How much of the time do we limit conversations to specific subjects or areas that we deem to be 'interesting' to ourselves and ignore all else, to our detriment? Too often, we write people and conversations off as being boring, not fitting in with our own fixed idea of what is, or is not, an interesting topic.

If you are prepared instead to engage in conversations with others whose life experiences or jobs are at odds with your own knowledge limitations, and are curious about acquiring new information from them, you will become a more enriched person. Someone whose knowledge about others and life itself will mushroom. In turn, you too will be able to share with and enrich others with the information gained as a result.

Some of us are naturally more curious than others, but most of us have to actively and consciously work on adding this skill to our armoury. Some of the most interesting conversations in my life have followed on from allowing myself to be actively curious, when engaged in a conversation with another person, about some area of interest about which I knew very little. If nothing else, the exercise that follows will demonstrate how little most of us really know about life, with its rich and endless variety. I strongly recommend that you engage with this exercise if you wish to improve your conversational skills.

Conversational Skills: Exercise Three
For one week, consciously focus your attention during every conversation that takes place between you and others, on developing your sense of curiosity about the topics or subjects of

discussion that take place during them. This requires a major conscious change in your thinking. You will need to empty your mind of all previous biases towards what seems interesting or not to you, relating to either the person or topic being discussed. Adopt the attitude of the child, who approaches much of what they see and hear, at a particular moment of time, with curiosity and wonder. How does that work? Why is that the colour or shape it is? Why do we have clouds in the sky? Why do we get rainbows?

Have you ever watched a small child stop and look at a ladybird, enthralled for moments as they observe what it is getting up to? They are teaching us something of great importance. Each one of us must try to learn something new every day about others, their lives and about life itself. We have to work on building up a repository of knowledge for the future. This is the attitude I wish you to adopt for this week and beyond.

This is another exercise that may seem strange, and often extremely challenging at the beginning. This is because the older we get, the greater the tendency to shut down our sense of curiosity. If, on the other hand, you really concentrate and show genuine interest and curiosity in what another person is revealing to you, it is amazing how much interesting information you can glean from such a conversation. After a while, you may notice how rapidly your curiosity will be piqued during a conversation, as you seek to add yet more fascinating information to your memory banks.

Once again, it might be useful to write in your diary if there were specific conversations when applying this exercise, that allowed you to open up a whole new world of information about some area, previously unknown to you. Did you feel excited about this discovery? Did you notice that the other person really enjoyed sharing the information with you as they sensed your interest and desire to learn more as a result? Do you feel that you are now opening up channels of knowledge previously denied to you by being fixed in your ways of thinking? Eventually, as with previous skills, if you keep working on and practising this skill, a sense of curiosity will become second nature to you, and in time you will be able to share information gained with others.

Skill Four: How to Practise Silence during a Conversation

In the previous chapter, we discussed the importance of introducing moments of silence during particular conversations. This might be appropriate where we are meeting someone who has lost a loved one. It might involve a desire to get an important point across, deciding that silence might be more effective than any words. It might be where you sense that staying silent might allow for a deeper conversation than any words expressed, or that a period of silence might get a point across more effectively than through any verbal comments.

But practising silence during a conversation is a difficult skill to acquire. It goes against our social nature to stay quiet in many situations. It is so much easier to fill a conversation with words, rather than leaving that awkward silence. Yet those who develop this skill, and the art of knowing when and how to use it, are frequently the most effective communicators. I would strongly recommend therefore that you take on the following exercise, aimed at teaching you how to effectively introduce silence into your conversational style.

Conversational Skills: Exercise Four
For one week, consciously focus your attention on actively introducing short periods of silence into conversations, where you deem it appropriate. It might be with a friend whom you

are chatting to, but sense that something is on their mind. You might ask some open question and then become silent to see what happens. It might be where you encounter someone who has lost a loved one, or where there has been a relationship breakup. You might open up with 'I don't know what to say to you,' followed by a period of silence. It might be a conversation where you really want to make a point about something of relevance, so perhaps verbally make the point, but follow it up with a period of silence to enforce your feelings. If you are observant and consciously focusing on the other person, you will notice how often introducing such a silence will facilitate the conversation to move to a deeper level, more so than with any expressed words.

This exercise is challenging, as most of us really struggle with the vacuum of silence during a conversation. In the beginning you may notice how every part of your being wants to break the silence, but consciously put a brake on your tongue and observe what happens when you do. After a while, you will begin to see the positive outcomes that develop and become more comfortable with longer periods of silence. Slowly but surely, you will notice how powerful a conversational tool silence is.

Once again, it can be helpful to write in your diary what your experiences of introducing silence into your conversations were. Did it seem very awkward in the beginning? When and where did you find it most effective? What were the obstacles you encountered? Are you finding it increasingly easier as time progresses?

If you continue to perform this exercise as part of your everyday conversations, you will gradually learn how to use silence as a natural conversational tool for the rest of your life.

Skill Five: How to Engage in Conversations in a Social Setting

This skill is primarily aimed at those who struggle with social anxiety or those who have difficulties with breaking into conversations in general. There will be a significant number of people, for example, with social anxiety, who find it extremely difficult to engage in conversations with either friends or strangers in a social situation. This can lead to much emotional distress for those affected.

If you find yourself in this group, then this exercise will give you some useful tools to bypass such difficulties. It is also a useful tool for us all, as it can often be quite intimidating to find yourself at a large work event, wedding ceremony or similar social situation, where you'll be faced with interacting with lots of people, including strangers. This skill is especially useful for any of us trapped in such a social situation, particularly if we are more introverted, who find it harder to initiate and maintain conversations in such circumstances. I use this exercise myself on a regular basis in social situations.

Some people find social conversations difficult, even awkward, especially in larger crowded situations. Their primary difficulty often lies in not knowing how best to break into a conversation with someone who is a stranger to them, as would often occur at weddings for example. Lacking any obvious information about the person and their lives, it can be difficult to know what topics are the best ones to begin with. In such situations, you, like the person with social anxiety, may feel a little embarrassed visualizing that the stranger you open up to may judge you harshly if you get it wrong.

Clearly, there are many people who do not share such concerns, especially extroverts. This group may be quite comfortable to launch into such conversations, and are even energized by them. If you are one of these, then the exercise that follows may not be of relevance to you, so feel free to progress to the next section.

For the rest of us, who may find these social situations more trying, then I strongly suggest the following conversation exercise.

At the heart of this exercise is an understanding that the only real topic that other people are most comfortable with and interested in discussing, during a conversation, is themselves, together with their lives, activities and hobbies. This is because most of us are in general self-obsessed. This is not a criticism, just an honest good-humoured appraisal of how we as human beings behave.

This insight suggests therefore that instead of having to find a topic that you hope others will find interesting, you encourage the other person to reveal to you what is of interest to them, namely something about themselves! In many ways, this exercise incorporates many of the principles contained in some of the exercises already discussed, in particular exercise three.

Let's see how this exercise will work in practice.

Conversational Skills: Exercise Five

For one week, apply the following conversation exercise in every social interaction you encounter with someone you know: ask them a question about some area of their lives that you know is of interest to them. It could be a query about their children if married, or a hobby or sport that they love, such as football, films, shopping, or whatever subject you know they love chatting about. Depending on their reply, ask them a further question and repeat the process until the person begins to naturally chat away about the topic they are so interested in. Once conversation about this topic begins to wane, shift to asking about another area you know they are interested in and repeat the process.

There is one absolute rule however when performing this exercise. You must, as discussed in exercise three, show intense interest in their replies. This is done through your non-verbal cues such as eye contact, facial expressions, hand movements etc. Their social brains are subtly hard-wired to pick up signs as to whether or not you are genuinely focusing on their answers. If you are not showing such interest, the other person will quickly shut down the conversation. This exercise requires a lot of energy and concentration to perform properly and will feel very strange in the beginning, but with constant practice, it becomes easier and easier to apply. Just like learning to drive a car!

But what about strangers, you might rightly ask, where you lack information about their life and areas of interest. How can you circumvent this difficulty? This is why so many of us struggle in larger social situations, where we are thrown into enforced contact with people we know little about. **The second part of this exercise will assist you to overcome this challenge.**

Let's say you are introduced to someone in the pub or at a party or work gathering. In such situations use the following three questions as entry points into conversation. The first is the typically Irish question 'Where do you come from?' The second is 'Where do you work?' or 'What are you studying?' The third is 'What do you do in your spare time?' or 'Do you have any hobbies?' I recommend the questions in that order.

It is extraordinary how long a conversation can go on for, based on these three simple questions. Once again, you can apply the same technique as above. Depending on the reply the person gives you, ask a further question and so on, all the time showing intense interest in their replies. Suppose the reply to the first question is 'I have just moved up from Cork to Dublin,' your next question might be 'Are you originally from Cork?' If they reply 'Yes,' the next question might be 'Do you still have family living there?' If the answer is yes, then you might go on to inquire who is in the family and so on.

Once you have exhausted question one, move on to question two and begin again. Suppose the reply to that question is 'I am studying nursing,'; the next question might be 'Where?' Depending on their reply you might ask 'And how are you finding the course?' and so on. Similarly, when you get to question three, where the potential for conversational topics is endless, you repeat the same process. Suppose the person replies 'I love hill walking,' you might ask 'Where is your favourite destination for walking?' or 'How did you get into hill walking?' and so on. The key again is, as discussed, you must show intense interest in their replies.

You may worry that others will think of you as strange or odd for asking so many questions. Keep in mind, however, that all human beings love to chat about themselves and their lives, so you are simply tapping in to this reality. Many people will not even notice what you are doing or will be 'chuffed' that you are taking such an interest in them, as long as you continue to completely focus your attention on them and their replies. They may even mention to their friends or loved ones just how 'interesting' a person you were to talk to!

The real secret to this exercise is to practise it on every person you meet, not only for the week in question but ideally for a longer period of time, until it becomes second nature to you. We can also learn so much information about so many areas of life about which we may know very little by using this exercise. This is because in the process of eliciting information, and if curious, as we discussed in the previous exercise, you will be adding to your own bank of knowledge about life.

Once again, be sure and document in your diary what you have learned from applying this exercise, especially on how, as time progresses, you are becoming more comfortable with using it.

Before leaving this section, let's see what happens to Vivienne and Ben when they decide for different reasons to develop their conversational skills.

Vivienne's Story

Vivienne is a thirty-three-year-old nurse who has been drifting in and out of relationships for the previous decade. A complete extrovert, she becomes energized by people, and cannot understand how others might find conversation difficult. It is something she lives for. What she fails to realize, however, is just how overwhelming a force she is during routine social conversations, or how this facet of her communication skills is actually impacting on her friendships and relationships. She has always tended to dominate conversations, as her two closest friends, Majella and June, can attest.

Majella, who, like most of the population, is somewhere in the middle of the introvert–extrovert scale, can cope with little difficulty with her friend's tendency to dominate conversations. For her, this is just a facet of her friend's personality and she accepts it, if finding it, on occasion, trying. June, however, her other close friend, is a complete introvert, who prefers to speak less and listen more, and who is more than comfortable with silence during a conversation. This aspect of June sometimes irks Vivienne who prefers to chat with others like herself, who revel in conversation. She is very fond of her two friends however and accepts that this is June's personality.

Then Vivienne's most recent relationship breaks down, the latest in a long line of such occurrences. She is chatting to Majella subsequently, querying why she seems unable to hold down a relationship for any period of time. How she often finds the guys in question boring. She also admits that, despite loving June to bits, she on occasion finds her equally boring. Majella feels it is time to share some home truths with her friend, even if Vivienne finds it difficult to hear them. They have a frank conversation, where Majella lays out her concerns that Vivienne is too dominant in conversations with others, who as a result are either intimidated, or simply become switched off, as they are uninterested in what she is conversing about. How her conversations are always about herself. She also suggests that perhaps guys were being put off by this facet of her behaviour and that she needs to work on her listening and conversational skills. Finally, Majella challenges Vivienne's use of the term 'boring'. Was it not the topic of a conversation that should be classified as boring, not the person themselves?

Vivienne is initially shocked by these revelations, but honest enough to realize that Majella is trying to be of assistance. Perhaps it is time to make some changes. Let's see what happens when she decides, with the assistance of a life coach, Martin, recommended by her friend, to put the conversational exercises and skills outlined into practice.

She begins, on Martin's advice, by consciously observing her conversational style over three days, and how it is affecting those with whom she is conversing. As she admits to Majella, what she discovers makes her squirm with embarrassment. She becomes increasingly aware how domineering she is during conversations. How she is only interested in topics or subjects of interest to herself, quickly shutting down any information flowing from the other person. She is even more affected by consciously observing the effects of this behaviour on others. For the first time, she begins to notice the 'glaze in their eyes' that seems to appear quite quickly on some occasions as she is speaking. She admits to Majella how she has noticed similar reactions in some of the men she has dated, and frequently wondered why. By the end of the three days, a chastened person, she is ready to make some serious changes.

For one week, on the advice of Martin, she begins the task of trying to focus on removing herself from being centre stage. This turns out to be one of the most challenging tasks she has ever set herself. She has to consciously sit on her natural tendency to rush in with her own comments or to switch the subject to something of interest to herself, on occasion having to literally bite her tongue. It takes all of her willpower to only focus on and converse about the topics or issues that the other person wants to chat about. But bit by bit, she notices that she is saying less and listening more. She also notices that people are no longer presenting with a glaze in their eyes and seem more interested in and buoyed by the conversation. This is an exercise, however, as she notes to Majella and in her diary, that she will have to continue working on for many weeks to come, but is determined to do so.

She then progresses to consciously, for a further week, showing as much interest during conversations as possible. She finds this equally difficult to practise as it is a foreign experience for her to consciously concentrate on anyone other than herself. She has to actively angle her face towards the person and works hard on making eye-to-eye contact, trying desperately to stay in the moment with them. As with focusing on the content of the other person's conversation however, she gradually begins to feel more comfortable doing this, even if once again she has to remind herself regularly to do so. She observes the positive effects that this is having on those she is conversing with, encouraging her to keep going.

With Martin's assistance, she then tackles the exercise she dreads most, namely having to develop her sense of curiosity about topics and issues that others with whom she is conversing find interesting. As she admits to Majella, she has always found her attention span, in relation to so many areas of life not of direct relevance to herself, extremely limited. This explains why she has found so many people boring in the past, especially in her personal relationships. She steels herself, however, and, for the following week, makes a conscious decision to not only focus on and show interest in topics brought up in conversations with others, but to become genuinely curious about the information that they share with her. She finds this extremely difficult in the beginning, but notices that the more she interrogates through the lens of curiosity, the more interesting she finds conversations becoming. This is most apparent when she chooses to chat to her friend June, someone whom she is very fond of, but with whom she has always struggled to find mutual areas of interest. June is fascinated by history and archaeology and is simply a fount of knowledge in these areas. To date, Vivienne would simply have switched off if June began to discuss some of her most recent findings in this area. Now she begins to have increasingly interesting chats with her friend, finding that the more she delves into these subjects with her, the more curious she is becoming about the whole area. This bonds the two of them much closer than before, deepening their friendship. As Vivienne comments to Majella at a later stage, 'Imagine that I thought that June was boring!'

By this stage, Vivienne is finding her whole take on conversations is changing rapidly and for the better. She is now ready to add silence to the mix, something neither she, nor anyone who knows her, could believe was possible. The idea of Vivienne remaining silent for any reason seemed impossible. But that is her next task, and over a one-week period and onwards, she tackles it with gusto.

She begins to consciously allow periods of silence to develop during conversations, where she deems it appropriate, especially if she senses that saying nothing at the time would either allow the other person time to gather their thoughts, or add weight to some observations she herself might make about information shared by them. As with most of these conversation exercises, it feels strange at first and she is extremely self-conscious. To her surprise, however, the responses to such periods of silence are often amazingly positive. Gradually, she becomes increasingly comfortable with the world of silence and its power, and vows to make it a regular part of her conversation armoury.

By the end of six weeks, the skills Vivienne has assiduously practised are bearing much fruit. Even those close to her notice the change. Gone is the non-stop chatter and the desire to over-power every conversation. Instead, she is gradually becoming a really interesting and empathetic conversationalist, someone whom others are increasingly drawn to chat to. The benefits don't just extend however to her close friends and associates. She sees a change in how guys she hooks up with now relate to her. How they are finding her increasingly easy to talk to. How she is listening more and saying less. It is now time to apply her new-found skills to the world of relationships and Majella has introduced her to a new colleague!

Ben's Story

Ben is twenty-six and for much of his teens and early twenties, he's suffered from severe social anxiety, which causes him untold emotional distress. He has always hoped that as he got older, and left college to enter the workforce, matters would right themselves.

Alas, as he is discovering, social anxiety often worsens, rather than improves, over time. His life is now spiralling out of control. He begins to increasingly dread social situations, from parties, to the pub, to the office canteen, in fact anywhere he is forced to interact with others. His worst nightmare is to find himself in a social situation where he will be asked to engage in conversation with a stranger, especially if of the opposite sex. At such times, his levels of anxiety and embarrassment rocket. His social anxiety difficulties are impacting severely on his ability to have relationships, and he finds himself increasingly stranded in the world of loneliness. Things get so bad sometimes that dark thoughts enter his mind, but he knows that his family would be destroyed if he acted on them so he battles on.

Finally, on the advice of a close friend, Robert, Ben agrees to work with a CBT therapist, and from that moment on his life begins to alter for the better. With her assistance and some targeted exercises, Ben begins to understand that social anxiety is more about his false perceptions of what happens in social situations rather than what in fact occurs in real life. His therapist persuades him to perform the Anxiety Inspector Exercise for a week. This is where he has to find evidence for her of other people demonstrating the physical signs of anxiety in social situations. Of course he struggles to find any, as such symptoms are impossible to see in real life. She also challenges the many unhelpful behavioural patterns that he has built up over the years, such as avoidance, excessive use of alcohol, staying at the edge of groups, face monitoring and the dread post-mortem following on from the social occasion.

But, as his therapist and indeed Ben himself admits, his primary difficulty in social situations lies in his paralysing fear of conversation. He feels tongue-tied at times, always unsure of what to say.

Worried that people would think he is weak or weird if they notice that his voice is shaky for example or that the topic he would choose to converse about will seem boring or stupid to them. He firmly believes that as a result of these conversational difficulties other people consider him personally boring and to be avoided at all costs. This of course only adds to his feelings of loneliness.

As he explains to his therapist, it is this block more than anything else that is preventing him from engaging in meaningful relationships with members of the opposite sex. He is simply paralysed in such situations and cannot see himself ever becoming comfortable conversing socially.

His therapist reassures him that this is an almost universal finding in social interactional anxiety. That there are, however, some simple conversational techniques that he can learn to apply, with a view towards breaking this logjam in his mind.

On further discussion, Ben admits that he really struggles to both initiate social conversations and find topics that others will find of interest. 'I spend so much time trying to initiate the conversation and then, on managing to do so, constantly monitoring their faces as I am talking,' he explains, 'trying to assess if they are finding me interesting, or a bore.'

This leads to a discussion on whether a person can be considered as boring or whether it is the topic of conversation that should be described as such. Ben finally admits that it is the topic of conversation rather than the human being that can be described as such.

To assist Ben to overcome his difficulties in this area, his therapist encourages him to begin with exercise six, discussed earlier. In the beginning he would perform this exercise with those close to him and then gradually widen it out to every social interaction, no matter how small, or whatever the setting is. He is to particularly focus on applying it to situations where he encounters someone of the opposite sex, and with strangers.

The weeks that follow are particularly challenging for Ben, for whom all of this approach is completely foreign, different to how he has approached conversations to date.

He begins by practising it with family and close friends at every opportunity, then gradually with work colleagues and with encounters in the service industry. He firstly asks people he knows about areas they are interested in, and really focuses on both their replies and suitable follow-on questions and on ensuring that he is showing intense interest in their replies. He requires some assistance from his therapist, in relation to eye-to-eye contact, for example, as this has always been a challenge for him. He becomes increasingly comfortable with this technique, gradually getting the hang of the exercise, and finds himself less stressed while carrying it out.

He progresses to applying the three questions outlined earlier, to conversations with strangers, something he goes out of his way to have, especially with those of the opposite sex. He is extremely anxious at the beginning, that they will think there is something wrong with him for asking all of these questions, that they will think he is strange or weird!

To his great surprise, however, the opposite occurs. He is astounded at how easy it is to facilitate others to talk about themselves and their lives, hobbies and activities, as long as he continues to show genuine interest. His therapist also discusses the importance of developing a sense of curiosity about others during this exercise, and he finds this happening naturally as time progresses.

By the end of twelve weeks, Ben cannot believe how quickly he has progressed from being tongue-tied to feeling extremely comfortable in any social situation in which he finds himself. He can now head straight into a group of strangers or people he knows and, with a judicious usage of the above questions, chat away without feeling any need to search for a suitable topic that others will find interesting. They are doing the work for him. As a result of all of his hard work, his social anxiety is rapidly disappearing. His loneliness is also beginning to dissipate. As Ben now shares with his therapist, his next task is to apply the conversational skills acquired to the world of relationships, and he already has his eyes on where he is going to start!

What the above two stories illustrate is just how important good conversational skills are, and how much they can enrich our everyday lives if applied correctly. If you can acquire them and base them on a solid foundation of active listening, you are well on your way to becoming an accomplished emotional connector.

Now that we have discussed in detail the importance of verbal skills in relation to emotional connection, let's explore the role of non-verbal strategies and skills (such as body language, mentioned briefly above).

PART THREE

WEEK 2:

WHAT DO YOU REALLY MEAN?

7. Non-verbal Communication Skills

In the previous section we briefly mentioned the importance of non-verbal communication skills. We have known for decades that the majority of communication occurring between human beings is non-verbal. It is likely that at least 65 to 70 per cent of all such communication is non-verbal and this figure may even be higher. This is not to say that verbal communication, as already discussed in the previous section, is not an essential part of our human existence. There is a body of opinion that believes that it was the advent of language that has allowed human beings to accelerate their progress in the last few thousand years to where we are today.

If you wish to become a really skilled emotional connector, however, it becomes necessary to explore a completely different form of communication, which is non-verbal in nature. At first glance it seems strange to be discussing a form of communication that does not include language, either spoken or aural. This is because most of us perform this type of networking every moment of the day, at a subliminal or unconscious level, sublimely unaware of its importance to our everyday lives. We are, for example, constantly picking up subtle non-verbal cues from other people and are often unaware that we too are sending out similar non-verbal signals to them. Those who spend time honing their non-verbal communication skills will reap rewards in terms of future social interactions both in the workplace and in the realm of interpersonal relationships in particular. Let's explore this concept further.

What is Non-verbal Communication?

Non-verbal communication relates to the manner in which human beings use non-verbal signals or cues to communicate with each other. These signals or cues include our facial expressions, eye gaze, tone of voice, body language and posture, and hand movements including touch and handshakes. While externals such as how we present ourselves in public in the form of clothes, hairstyle, footwear and cosmetics are obviously forms of non-verbal communication (as they are telling the other person something about ourselves), it is the more subtle cues detailed above that we are really interested in here.

As already discussed in chapter two, the social brain is incredibly attuned to picking up these unconscious, subliminal signals from those whom we come in contact with, in routine face-to-face encounters. It is vital, however, to understand from the beginning that this is a two-way conversation. Your social brain is picking up so many cues from their non-verbal cues, but so too is their social brain, picking up information from the unconscious signals that you too are emanating. This latter point is often completely overlooked when discussing this form of communication.

Non-verbal communication is frequently occurring at the same time as you are verbally interacting with another person. It is as if there are two separate parallel conversations occurring during such interactions. The first one relates to the conscious action of conversing and listening to the other person and vice versa. The second conversation is happening subconsciously at the same time, with each person subtly, and at incredibly fast speeds, internally monitoring all of the non-verbal cues emanating from the other.

In the main, these two communication systems are in harmony. In such situations, the verbal messages being sent out are backed up by the subliminal non-verbal messages. We have not consciously focused our attention on the latter, it just happens automatically. Let's suppose for example that you are verbally communicating to a friend or work colleague how sorry you were to hear of the death of their mother. Since both the spoken words and non-verbal cues such as the warm hug or embrace, together with all of the other signals emanating from you, are in harmony, this social interaction may bring both of you closer together, from that moment on.

There will be occasions, however, where the two communication systems are in disharmony and internal warning bells go off. Something just doesn't feel right here. We find ourselves subtly backing off the conversation or becoming more wary of the other person, often for no conscious reason that we can put our finger on. This is because our non-verbal system is noticing small subtle cues that seem off, and sending warning signals from our social brain to take action accordingly.

Suppose you are a woman in your mid-twenties and you meet up with a guy at a party who seems to be saying all the right things and who is suggesting a further date. You find however that your non-verbal communication system is screaming at you, with your social brain sending out warnings, that there seems to be something 'off' about the person, despite his smooth urbane conversational style. You may not even be aware of what the disconnect is. It may be something in his body language or his facial expression that is triggering alarm bells. Internally, your social brain unconsciously encourages you to shut down this conversation and withdraw. Most of us can relate to similar experiences in our social world. This fascinating world of non-verbal communication is worthy of a book on its own and a discipline has actually grown up to study it, called kinesics. (This term refers to the study of hand, arm, body and face movements and their role in how we communicate with each other, through facial expressions, body language etc.)

Let's explore the main non-verbal communication cues of relevance in becoming a skilled emotional connector. In the subsequent chapter we will then explore how you can improve your skills in this area. We will be examining the importance of facial expressions, eye movements, body language and posture (including hand and head gestures), touch, and finally personal space.

One might ask why we are not including body presentation props, such as clothes or cosmetics, in this section. While we can definitely change our appearance and send out different non-verbal cues by engaging in such a process, I have chosen to exclude such props, focusing instead on those cues which I believe are universal to all of us irrespective of culture or fashion.

Facial Expressions

We rarely focus consciously on our facial expressions, yet much of how we connect and communicate with each other is bound up with them. Every moment of the day, your facial expressions are constantly changing, depending on the emotions or circumstances you encounter.

There is a particularly strong link between your emotional world and your facial expressions, and it is now recognized that one can strongly influence the other. If your facial expressions are downbeat, you may feel more depressed or sad. If you consciously encourage your facial muscles to smile, you can actually lift your mood. If you feel sad or depressed, your facial expressions will either be downbeat or in the case of the latter, almost frozen. So too, if you are happy or joyful, your face will light up.

Facial expressions are created by the fine muscles around the face, eyes, forehead and mouth being activated, especially during a conversation with another person. They can reveal so much subtle additional information to others and indeed to yourself, separate to the words being expressed. Once again, it is a two-way conversation that is going on. Facial expressions can let us know if either person in a conversation is tired, excited, anxious, angry, depressed, frustrated, sad, confident, smug, shy, or even bored. All of this data is being accessed and reviewed by our social brains at the most amazing of speeds, with unconscious conclusions being made, based on the information received. What we often fail to recognize is how much of our social decision-making is being influenced by this process. The greatest dilemma for our social brain occurs when the facial expressions being picked up are not in harmony with the words or emotions being expressed. We may find ourselves feeling socially uneasy, without really understanding just why.

Common emotions that influence our facial expressions are fear, anger or frustration, sadness, depression, joy or happiness and disgust. So much information is passed from one person to another for example through a smile, a frown, a grimace or, on some occasions, muscles contorted by fear or worry.

Smiling is an especially important facial expression in relation to emotional connection. How we smile will say a lot about us. Is it a warm, all-embracing smile or just a grimace? Does it carry a hint of mockery or disdain? Is there a coldness to the facial expressions when the person smiles? Does the smile reach their eyes? This is relevant, because we smile not just with our facial expressions, but also with our eyes, which we will explore later. As human beings, our social brain can quickly sense how genuine or not a smile is. It is especially wary of the person whose smile never reaches their eyes. Yet, how many of us ever focus consciously on this key facial expression, which conveys so much information about us to others?

Those who are encountering two key mental health difficulties, namely social anxiety and depression, are especially vulnerable in the area of facial expressions and the common link is the amygdala. This is because our amygdala in the emotional brain is hard-wired to focus on emotional expressions, especially fear and depression. Someone with social anxiety, for example, often misreads facial expressions of those they encounter in social situations, believing that the person is judging them as being anxious, weak and weird. This is why they spend so much time face-monitoring contacts in social situations.

Bouts of depression (the illness) have long been associated with either a lack of facial expressions at all in social situations or else with more downbeat expressions. There is also a predisposition for a person with this illness to pick out others who are also feeling sad or down in a social situation and to misread the facial expressions of those they come in contact with, therefore falsely believing the other person is either bored with them or else not comfortable being around them. They tend to have a bias towards the facial expressions of sadness or depression. For example, if you give a person with depression a list of facial expressions that include such emotions, and ask them to pick one at random, they will usually zone in on the depressed face.

When both of these conditions are successfully treated, and the amygdala is back in its box, we are able to read facial expressions more effectively.

It is not only some mental health conditions that can have a direct effect on our normal facial expressions. Some neurological conditions, especially Parkinson's disease, and strokes affecting one or other side of the face, can lead to the facial muscles affected struggling to respond naturally during conversations. In the former condition, for example, the lack of facial reactions during routine social interactions is often a warning symptom of the emergence of this condition, even before the person's gait becomes affected.

Another routine procedure that can also seriously affect our natural facial expressions and spontaneity is that of injecting Botox into facial muscles. While leading to a smoother, younger complexion, this procedure unfortunately also has the side effect of making it harder to express and read our natural facial expressions. So too with plastic surgery involving the face. Once again, if overdone, this can make our skin so stretched that all natural expressions are negatively affected.

All of this information demonstrates just how important your natural unconscious facial expressions are. Time spent focusing on them will greatly assist you in your task of becoming an emotional connector. Above all, your facial expressions need to be genuine, and in harmony with the messages you are either imparting or receiving. Some of you may be already doing this automatically, having over the years become unconsciously skilled at this. It is a real art for example to be able to 'control' your facial expressions, so as not to reveal your true emotional reactions to some information being imparted. Some cultures, such as the Chinese and the Japanese, pride themselves on developing this skill and use it to great advantage for example in business negotiations. While it can be useful to acquire this ability, there is an associated risk that we may in the process remove much of the human warmth and empathy that flows from genuine facial expressions of emotions during conversations.

There will be many of us, however, who are probably totally unaware of the importance of facial expressions at all, and who would benefit greatly from both recognizing them and learning how to use them to our advantage.

Later, we will be exploring some exercises to assist you to do just that.

Eye Contact

In many ways, your eyes are the most expressive of all of the body parts associated with non-verbal communication. The saying that 'the eyes are the window to the soul', the origin of which is obscure, is indeed accurate. It suggests that we can, by staring into the eyes of another person, make a reasonable guess at the emotions they are feeling at that moment in time. We can say, or not say, so much with our eyes. This is why eye contact is one of the core non-verbal forms of communication, frequently more powerful emotionally than any words expressed.

Eye contact during conversations has so many different functions. Through your eyes, you can convey and receive vital information both emotionally and contextually. Almost a third of your brain is taken up with analysing the visual information flowing in from your eyes. They convey this vital information about the world around you to the visual processing part of the cortex, which in turn shares it with social and emotional parts of your brain.

Eye contact also allows you to convey information to another person, without any other form of verbal communication. We all can recognize for example that 'look' that our mother or father might have given us as a child, to cease whatever mischief we were up to; or the 'look' that one might share with one's partner, suggesting that it is time to leave the party or social event. In both of these examples, words were unnecessary; simple eye contact was all that was required.

You can also convey other subtle messages with a simple glance. How you are upset, angry, hurt, anxious, bored, are finding something humorous, or agree or disagree with something that has been said, often without the assistance of the spoken word. When we are directly conversing with others, eye contact allows us, amongst multiple functions, to interpret the emotional impact of what is being said, whether the words match the non-verbal cues, whether the other person is on the same wavelength as us, and their sincerity. How often do we unconsciously avoid eye contact for example to discourage people socially from coming near us or to avoid specific social interactions? While this may on occasion be useful, it is important to not allow this pattern to become the norm for you.

I have always believed that the presence or absence of genuine eye-to-eye contact is the key to real emotional connection. For direct eye-to-eye contact, along with sincerity and warmth, will often break down major barriers to communication. This is because the emotional and social brain is so hard-wired to sense any falseness, or lack of real interest or empathy through its eye-to-eye assessments, that it will automatically pick up such negative cues and react by shutting down such social interactions.

This is why it is so important in social situations to keep our gaze naturally on the other person as much as possible, something that so many of us are not especially skilled at. We can also say so much with our eyes, conveying so many messages that we might otherwise feel unable to communicate. In relation to emotional connection, the 'eyes' rather than the 'I's have it!

Once again, we will be exploring some techniques later to assist you in developing such skills.

Body Language and Posture

Another area of non-verbal communication that many of us remain unaware of is the world of body language and posture. How often do you pay attention to the posture you adopt when communicating with someone else? Yet their internal social brain picks up vital information when you for example fold your arms and hands in front of you as opposed to keeping them open and relaxed. The former posture suggests either that you are unhappy with the nature of the conversation or else that you are remaining shut down to receiving or accepting what another person is saying to you. The latter posture suggests that you are open, friendly and receptive to new information. All of this information being processed quietly and seamlessly, without a word being spoken about your attitude to the other person! It can be chastening to realize that your posture, whether sitting or standing when having such conversations, is revealing a lot about you to the other person. Thankfully, this form of communication is bi-directional, so you too are learning much about them through a similar process.

Suppose you are sitting down and leaning forward as the person is chatting to you, then this might suggest that you are showing real interest in what they are saying to you. On the other hand, lolling back in the chair might suggest the opposite, that you are bored or indifferent. Suppose your head movements are tilted towards the person; this again might show interest, while tilted away, looking down at the ground or, even worse, looking over their shoulder, might strongly suggest you are bored or disinterested. Even a simple nod towards someone can convey different meanings, depending on how it is done. A curt nod might suggest a desire to have little further to do with the person, whereas a gentle nod towards someone might be seen as a greeting.

How you stand, or the posture you adopt when having a conversation, will also reveal much. There is something, for example, about encountering a person with both hands on their hips that irritates many of us. This is because it suggests that the person feels the need to assert themselves over us, and instinctively this can make us feel uncomfortable or even annoyed. On the other hand, if you are having a chat with someone, and they are busily using their hands in a natural way to make a point, this suggests that they are engaged in the conversation emotionally. If the person has both hands in their pockets, this can suggest that either they are quite relaxed in your company, or sometimes only half listening, and your social brain will be busy seeking out further clues as to which one it is.

All of us have unconscious automatic body language and posture habits. Whether we constantly fidget when conversing, are avid hand gesture users, or tend to cross our legs when sitting and chatting to someone, all of these movements say something about us. It is only when you either video yourself in action or consciously focus your attention on what your individual patterns are that you can truly build up a picture of how you communicate through posture, head and hand gestures.

Touch

One of the lasting memories of the Covid pandemic, one that will live long in the memories of those of us who have lived through it, is a new respect and understanding of the importance of touch as a form of communication. Family members and loved ones could not embrace each other in a normal way. Friends could not shake hands or hug each other. Loved ones dying in hospital passed away often on their own, lacking that final desperate clinging hug, to send them on their way. We could not embrace the dead body or friends and loved ones at the wake. All of this was so foreign to us as human beings. From time immemorial, one of the most important forms of non-verbal communication has been touch. There is even a discipline called haptics, exploring how we connect using touch.

Most of us are either 'huggers' or 'non-huggers'. This suggests that some of us are comfortable using an embrace or hug as an important means of communicating to the other person how we feel about them. Others are more comfortable with a simple handshake, which, as we will see, can also tell us so much about a person. There is also a strong cultural dimension to this form of non-verbal communication. For example, in countries such as Japan, a simple bow would go a lot further than any attempt to show affection through a hug or a handshake. Move to a Mediterranean country such as Italy, France or Spain and the opposite applies, with hugs and kisses being seen as a normal manner of greeting.

Most of the time we tend to use a hug to show real affection to a close friend, family member or someone with whom we feel genuinely comfortable, whether that be a business colleague, fellow professional, or a casual friend whom we might meet on a regular basis. Such hugs or embraces might be a quick gesture or more prolonged, depending on how close the person is to us. Sometimes it might take the form of a simple pat on the back to show the person that you are there for them or are glad to see them. On other occasions you might use a mix of both a hug and a pat. There are obviously different types of hugs, from the common, so-called crisscross hug, where one person's arms are above or below the other's, to the real bear hug type of embrace, which is often tinged with excitement at seeing the person. As a general rule of thumb, the closer the relationship you have with the person, the deeper and longer the hug will be. Clearly, embracing someone in a romantic or personal relationship does not fall into this discussion, as the connotations of such a hug may be more complex. Here we are more interested in routine normal social interactional situations.

Our social brains are extremely adept at sensing whether a hug or embrace is appropriate or not in a social interaction and will react accordingly. This is because we are also noticing lots of other cues, which tell us if it feels right or not. If the latter, you may feel uncomfortable and find yourself instinctively pulling away from the person. Culture will obviously play a role here, as already discussed.

Another important form of touch relates to the simple handshake. In many social and working situations and for people who do not feel comfortable with a quick hug, a handshake may be a more appropriate gesture. Once again, we can learn so much unconsciously from the simple act of shaking hands. Our social brain is simply gobbling up information about a person at lightning-fast speed, every time we shake someone's hand in a social or working situation. So, what can we learn?

A firm handshake would suggest that the person you are dealing with is more extrovert, open, interested in meeting you and self-confident. A limp handshake may suggest the opposite, that they are more introverted, less confident or perhaps less interested in having a meaningful conversation with you. This once again is a two-way conversation, as they are also learning much about you via your handshake. Their social brain is also assessing other key non-verbal signals such as your posture, eye gaze and facial expressions, coming to a rapid judgement of you as someone they can either trust and like, or someone they feel less comfortable with.

If you try to overdo the firm handshake however, this may send out different signals, namely that you are either less confident in yourself or wish to dominate the conversation, neither of which is useful for emotional connection. Some people like to use both hands to clasp the other person's hand when meeting them. Depending on the other non-verbal signals being registered by the social brain, this form of handshake, if felt to be genuine, can make the other person feel especially valued.

The length of time that you hold someone's hand can also be of great importance. Hold it for too long and it may be regarded as being too familiar, too short and it may suggest lack of respect! The ideal time is regarded as two seconds. Clearly, there will be exceptions to this, as, for example, if greeting a close friend who has lost a loved one to cancer. Here it might feel completely appropriate to hold their hand for a much longer period of time. This is because other non-verbal signs being picked up by their social brain will suggest that you are doing this because you genuinely care.

The Importance of Personal Space

How often has it happened to each one of us that someone, often with the best of intentions, invades our personal space, triggering alarm bells in our social brain? Few of us ever really consider, when having a conversation with someone, just what is an appropriate space to leave between ourselves and the other person. Yet personal spacing is once again an important non-verbal signal that we need to pay attention to. The discipline associated with studying this phenomenon is called proxemics, and it explores how space or distance influence communication.

Proxemics theory was begun in the 1960s by anthropologist Edward T. Hall. He classified four degrees of interpersonal distance, or degrees of proximity, that we all experience. These four zones describe what is considered normal acceptable distance between one another, when communicating. These proxemic distances are: public (12 feet to 25 feet), social (4 to 12 feet+), personal (1 ½ to 4 feet) and intimate (less than 1 ½ feet). Interestingly, these zones are seen as elliptical rather than circular, as we take up more space in front of us, where our line of sight is, than at the side or back, where we are unable to monitor what people are doing.

When dealing with a public proxemic distance, you may have to speak louder to be heard, and it may become difficult to maintain direct eye contact, so the connection between two people is minimal. For the purpose of our discussion we are more interested in the social, personal and intimate distances, as these form the basis of our routine human social interactions. Let's explore these three proxemic distances in greater detail.

Social distance spacing is appropriate during our routine working, professional or casual social conversations, where the ideal distance from each other should be somewhere between four and six feet. The term keeping someone at 'arm's length' captures this distance really well. Imagine that you and the person you were speaking to stretched out your arms so hands barely touched and you will get a rough sense of this distance.

In social situations, we feel comfortable chatting away at this distance or space. If someone from this group however begins to move too close, your social brain will send out warning signals that they are 'invading your personal space'. Your natural response in such circumstances may be to either back away, or quickly shut down the conversation. This is because your social brain is feeling uncomfortable. Remember, this is a two-way non-verbal conversation, so you too need to be careful of not invading another person's social space, or you will trigger a similar response from their social brain.

Personal distance spacing is appropriate when communicating with those who are of greater significance in our lives. For example, we feel comfortable allowing friends or acquaintances of note to come closer to us, for a more intimate conversation. In this situation, the ideal distance between us and them lies somewhere between one and a half and four feet, where our social brain feels that this is appropriate. Once again, if this personal space is invaded, with the person coming too close, our social brain will unconsciously send out warning signals and we will behave accordingly.

Intimate distance spacing is appropriate when communicating with those whom we are closest to, namely our family, close friends and of course partners.

This ideal space is usually seen as one and a half feet and less. This is our true personal space, and we are especially sensitive if others breach this space. There are reasons for this, for this is the space in which we feel free to let our guard down, to be ourselves, to hug or embrace each other, all of which are so vital for our emotional nourishment.

It is important to be aware of personal space, both our own and others'. We regularly fail to consciously notice how far away from or how close we are to other people, or how they in turn are responding to our actions. It is all going on in our unconscious social brain, which is picking up strong non-verbal signals if someone does invade what it perceives as the appropriate social distance for that interaction. Most of us can relate to how this feels!

A skilled emotional connector will, however, have developed the skill of consciously ensuring that these personal space invasions do not happen. Their non-verbal messages as a result will be interpreted by the other person at an unconscious level as showing respect, and caring for their feelings. We will be exploring how to achieve this in the chapter that follows.

In summary, there is a whole world of communication going on, completely independent of the verbal messages we are passing back and forth during a routine conversation. Those who become skilled in this more subtle form of non-verbal messaging are clearly going to have a major advantage over those who choose to ignore it. If you would like to join this group of hotshot emotional communicators, then read on, as the next chapter will show you how to access the necessary skills to do just that.

8. How to Improve Your Non-verbal Communication Skills

The most obvious difficulty facing us when seeking to improve our non-verbal communication skills is that much of this messaging is going on unconsciously or subliminally. It is as if the social brain of one person is having a quiet chat with the social brain of another person, completely independently of the verbal messages passing between both parties. As discussed in the previous chapter, such internal messaging is happening primarily through the language of non-verbal cues, which most of us are completely oblivious to. We therefore have a conundrum on our hands. If it is happening unconsciously, how can you develop the necessary skills to improve your non-verbal networking? The answer lies in the extraordinary capacity of your brain to focus consciously on anything that you choose to designate as a priority, and also in its amazing ability, as already discussed in chapter two, to change its connections and pathways to learn new skills.

Your rational brain, specifically the prefrontal cortex, if you choose to prioritize something, has the ability to shine a light on the area in question, study it, learn from it and, if you decide, make changes. The key word here is choice. You will have to actively choose to prioritize an area and continue to focus on it for a reasonable period of time if you wish to make such changes.

What makes us humans so unique is our capacity to explore consciously what has previously been an unconscious process. It is this extraordinary ability of your brain that we are now going to tap in to. It is going to allow you to consciously shine a light on each of the non-verbal cues discussed in the last chapter. With the information revealed through this process, you can then consciously make efforts to improve your current skills in this area. With constant repetition of such skills, you can improve your non-verbal communication skills until gradually you find yourself applying them unconsciously.

What an amazing thought. By consciously choosing to prioritize learning about your unconscious non-verbal cues or messages, you can, if you deem it necessary, make some conscious changes or improvements to them. Then, through constant practice at integrating such changes into your everyday conversations, you can reach a point where this happens automatically or unconsciously. Your extraordinary social brain can take you on such a journey. All you have to do is make the choice to consciously prioritize each of the cues that make up your non-verbal communication system, discover how you are applying them, make whatever changes are deemed necessary and then see where this leads you. This can be a really exciting, life-transforming journey to make. If still on board, read on.

As detailed in the last chapter, the five non-verbal domains of interest to us are facial expressions, eye contact, body language and posture, touch and, finally, personal space. It is important from the outset to introduce the word 'harmony', for that is what we are trying to achieve. What we mean by this is ensuring that each of your non-verbal domains are aligned with the verbal or non-verbal messages you are trying to convey. This is the real key to effective emotional connection.

Our social brains are extremely adept at picking up disharmony between what we are saying verbally and what we are, or are not, saying non-verbally. While we will explore each of these domains separately, it is important to recognize that each one feeds into the next. What your social brain finally puts together is a composite picture, created from information from all five areas, of whether such harmony exists or not. It is our task to ensure that it does.

Skill One: How to Harmonize Your Facial Expressions

In the previous chapter, we noted how your facial expressions are intimately bound up with the emotions you are feeling at that moment in time, especially while conversing with another party. Since your emotions are constantly changing during such conversations every moment of the day, so too are your facial expressions. The key is whether or not such expressions are in harmony with the conversation in hand. Since we rarely, if ever, focus on our facial expressions at all, few of us are aware of whether such harmony is present or not in our social interactions with others.

Many stage and movie actors spend hours in front of a mirror, consciously trying to perfect all of the facial expressions associated with emotions such as sadness, depression, joy or happiness, fear or anxiety, anger or frustration, and disgust. The great actors are those whose facial expressions seem completely authentic to the character they are playing. They literally become the person. The key word here is authenticity. None of us, however, has the time or perseverance to spend hours in front of a mirror to ensure that our expressions are in harmony with our emotions. Some might even consider such exercises artificial or contrived. But we can certainly focus on consciously recognising whether or not we are being authentic in relation to facially expressing how we feel emotionally. This requires us to open ourselves up to others, to become more emotionally vulnerable. Paradoxically, it is so much easier to connect with and feel closer to someone who is confident enough to demonstrate such vulnerability and authenticity. Why? Because deep down, all of us as human beings feel the same! We can also seek out evidence of such authenticity in others with whom we are communicating. Here are a few simple exercises to do, to improve your skills in this area.

Non-verbal Cues: Exercise One

This exercise is aimed at ensuring that you are consciously focusing on being completely authentic in relation to your facial expressions. **For one week, when conversing with others in your everyday working or social life, focus on allowing your facial expressions to melt into the emotion that you are feeling at that moment in time.** Unless, for some reason, you are consciously trying to keep your facial expressions neutral for some personal or pragmatic reason, just allow yourself to express the emotion you are feeling at the time via your facial movements.

If feeling emotionally sad or happy, anxious or frustrated, depressed or joyful when communicating with another person, then be yourself and allow the muscles of your face to show how you are feeling internally. You are not being authentic if you are constantly trying to mask the facial expression of such emotions. The reality is that the other person's social brain will often sense when such cues are off and behave accordingly. You will usually discover that these emotions are being triggered by issues coming up in the conversation. Focus on some key areas of the face, especially your eyebrows, forehead and mouth, as these are the parts of the face that are most expressive. Simply lifting one or the other eyebrow can suggest so many things emotionally from surprise to disbelief to keen interest. Keeping your lips tightly pursed together can convey that you are angry and vice versa. Of all your facial expressions, work hardest on your smile, making sure that it is, if appropriate, warm and genuine. Often a simple smile can be more effective and say more about you as a person from a non-verbal perspective than all of the words that you could express. We will discuss this further when dealing with eye contact.

It requires a lot of intense, mindful focus to express yourself in this way, especially if you are someone who has always tried to hide your emotions. This exercise can however be summed up in two words: 'be yourself'. If you are prepared to be open and vulnerable through your facial expressions, you will find emotional connection immensely more satisfying and successful.

There will clearly be occasions when it will be inappropriate to demonstrate such emotions through your facial expressions. This will require you putting on a more neutral facial expression. But this should be a conscious decision, which is being made for some practical social or working reason. You might not wish to demonstrate much emotion, for example, if an important business decision is being made, for fear that you might be showing your hand in doing so. You might be hurt over something someone said inadvertently, but wish to withdraw for a short period to get your thoughts together before dealing with the situation, so decide to keep your facial expressions neutral during the initial conversation. The important word here is conscious. It is you consciously deciding not to show your emotions externally. In this way, you are still being authentically yourself.

If you are someone who has always tried to keep a tight rein on expressing your emotions, this exercise can be especially challenging. You may have always unconsciously kept your expression blank or maintained a neutral facial expression, come what may. In such situations you may find it helpful to enlist the help of a trusted friend, who can feed back to you whether your facial expressions are matching the emotions being expressed. You could, with their assistance, even take a video of both of you chatting about different topics. This can be especially helpful in allowing you to see yourself in action emotionally. One look can be worth a thousand words. It can be quite revealing to see yourself in action, and this can assist you to make further conscious changes to your expressions.

Your facial expressions however must not simply be in harmony with the emotion you are feeling at the time. They must also be in harmony with what the other person is sharing with you. If they are sharing something sad, such as the loss of a loved one, or the breakup of a relationship that has deeply affected them, it is key that your facial expressions are in harmony with theirs. If you are simply saying the words of condolence, but your facial expressions are not in harmony with these words, their social brain will sense it immediately and shut down. We will be discussing this concept in greater detail when dealing with empathy.

Skill Two: How to Make Genuine Eye Contact

Like facial expressions, eye contact is another critical non-verbal form of communication and the two cues go hand in hand. This is because they reveal so much about us at a subliminal level. If your eye contact and facial expressions are not in harmony, then the other person's social brain will immediately zone in on the discrepancy. So too, if the words being expressed are not in harmony with the emotional cues emanating from your eyes, trouble beckons for similar reasons. Rarely, however, do we focus consciously on eye contact as being of relevance when networking. Making sure for example that our eyes are in harmony with how we smile. That the emotions being expressed are backed up by the messages coming from our eye contact with the other person. That we are even making proper eye contact at all with them. How often do we consciously use eye contact to convey specific non-verbal messages?

There are also some practical issues involved in developing good eye contact skills. For example, how long should we maintain direct eye contact for? Should we focus our eyes on their eyes or on some other part of the face? Should we vary the pattern? How can we ensure that the other person feels comfortable with us, through eye contact? How important is smiling with our eyes?

Spending time on developing how best to use eye contact is therefore a really good idea. If you don't, you run the risk of your eyes letting you down non-verbally if not in harmony with the messages you are trying to convey, either verbally or through some other non-verbal cues. The social brain takes information coming in from eye contact very seriously, as it often reveals much of what you really believe or feel about something.

Non-verbal Cues: Exercise Two

For one week, I want you to consciously pay attention during every conversation on initiating and maintaining good eye contact with the person with whom you are conversing, using the following guidelines.

1. **Focus eye contact more when listening**, as it is the more important task, so spend about 70 per cent of the time focusing on eye-to-eye contact during this form of

communication. While conversing, a figure of 50 per cent of the time focusing on eye contact is more appropriate.

2. **Make eye contact, openly and squarely, with the person with whom you are conversing at the beginning of the conversation**. This is especially important in emotional connection as this is the 'make or break' moment, where others will make unconscious, lightning-fast assessments of you, depending on what they see. Make sure you maintain such eye contact for at least ten to fifteen seconds, especially if listening, as this sets the tone of the conversation immediately.

3. **Be especially careful with initial contact, not to look down or to the side of the person or, even worse, look over their shoulder** (the politician's gaze), as this can suggest a lack of interest, boredom, or shyness. Such basic errors in eye contact can destroy your emotional connection possibilities.

4. **Limit direct eye contact.** It can vary from person to person, but ideally continuous direct eye-to-eye contact in real life should only last around ten to fifteen seconds before shifting, and in general should not last longer than sixty seconds. Beyond this will often feel uncomfortable for both people in the conversation. Gazing at or focusing consciously on an area between or just above or below both eyes, say the bridge of the nose or the eyebrows, even the mouth, for some of the time, is easier to maintain than, and is just as effective as, direct eye-to-eye contact. It also feels more comfortable for both parties involved.

5. **Always shift your eye contact gradually and subtly.** Notice how your eyes instinctively drift from one spot to

another in the areas mentioned above every ten seconds or so and how this is a natural process.

6. **Pay particular attention to the part your eyes play in smiling.** You can smile with your face, with the warmth never reaching your eyes, for example, and this is a red flag to the social brain of the person you are networking with. A warm smile, especially when it reaches your eyes, suggests openness and is one of the real shortcuts to making the other person's social brain feel immediately at ease. This in turn will trigger them to relax in your presence and often to reveal more intimate information to you.

A real smile, where appropriate, combines both facial expressions and eye contact, and has the potential to pierce the heart of the most hardened individual. If it seems forced or artificial in nature, however, a smile can be completely misinterpreted by the other person and their social brain as being false, and will lead them to think that you are not trustworthy.

A genuine smile, on the other hand, suggests that you are open, vulnerable and authentic. It suggests that you are confident in yourself, that you are not taking yourself or life too seriously and that you are enjoying the company of the person in question. A powerful non-verbal message indeed.

7. **Simple eye contact movements can often suggest more in real life than the longest of conversations.** That 'look' for example that a spouse might make to suggest to the other that they are uncomfortable in a situation and would prefer to leave; or that one is interested romantically; or that it might be better to drop a topic seen as potentially awkward and so on. Practise them and see.

Skill Three: How to Improve Your Body Language and Posture

Having developed and practised new strategies in relation to your facial expressions and eye contact while conversing, it is now time to improve your body language and posture communication. We have already discussed their importance in the previous chapter. How your body posture – sitting or standing – hand gestures, placing of arms, hands or feet, can disclose so much non-verbal information about you. How often these are contradicting what you are saying verbally, thus, not in harmony. We are particularly interested in ensuring that you become more conscious of such movements and change any bad habits that may have crept in. In the process, we hope to harmonize your body language and posture with your verbal communications, to make you a better connector. One of the principal difficulties that all of us encounter in the area of body language and posture is how consciously un-aware of them we are during routine conversations.

Non-verbal Cues: Exercise Three
Your first task is to consciously focus attention for one week on your body language and posture during routine conver-sations. To achieve this objective, the best approach by far is to ask a friend, partner or work colleague to video you (say on their smartphone) during a number of conversations with others, or to watch videos of yourself giving talks or having social or working chats with others. This can be an amazing experience and if you have never done so, I strongly recommend this exercise to all. It is astonishing how much you will learn about your body language, posture, hand movements, gestures and so on, by simply observ-ing yourself in action.

Detail in your diary any characteristic, unconscious patterns that you adopt. Here are some examples of body language you might find you do:

- lean back in the chair or sit too upright
- either never use your arms or hands in conversation or (more likely) use them excessively
- tend to keep your hands in your pockets, relaxed by your sides or, more ominously, constantly fold them in front of you almost hugging yourself (this is a real body language statement that you are a closed system who is quite suspicious of people in general)
- either keep both legs straight out in front of you or constantly crossed
- constantly fidget with your hands
- lean in when chatting to someone, which shows genuine interest, or the opposite
- try to convey a sense of power or dominance, through adopting a wide stance, or vice versa
- tilt your head to show interest in a conversation, or perhaps you simply look at the ground.

It is also extremely useful to assess whether your body language and posture seem to be in harmony with the verbal messages you are sending out or are conflicting. If for example you are seemingly verbally agreeing with the person you are chatting to, but at the same time folding your arms tightly in front of you, then their social brain will pick up the mixed messages and become more guarded.

There is a wealth of information to be gained through this exercise, as all of us have idiosyncratic habits, which have often unconsciously built up over years, some of which are useful, but many of which are not.

It can also be useful to watch videos of other people, especially those you admire and would like to emulate, as they seem so comfortable when communicating with others. Watch out for many of the cues that we have discussed above and see how they compare to what you are doing. Are there any changes that you would now like to make to your own cues in this area?

Also during this week, consciously focus during every conversation on ensuring that you accentuate some of the positive messages learned from your video work in the previous exercise. Begin to challenge some of your negative behaviours. This might mean ensuring that your posture is neither too rigid nor too slouched, just comfortable. It could involve ceasing to cross your arms in front of you as an automatic habit or calming down those frantic hand gestures or movements or ceasing to constantly fidget with a pen or other item and so on. Maybe you could cease adopting a dominant or submissive pose, beginning instead to focus more on gently tilting your head towards a person during a conversation. Maybe it's time to take those hands out of your pockets!

If you do find yourself in the presence of someone whose body language and posture you have always admired, don't be afraid to consciously mirror what they are doing. Not only will you be practising your own non-verbal cues by doing this, but also unconsciously building in more positive ones, while indirectly making the other person subliminally feel more at home with you, through these actions.

Skill Four: How to Harness the Power of Touch

Touch, as discussed in the previous chapter, reveals so much about us from a non-verbal perspective. Our emotional and social selves desperately need touch both to nourish us and as a means of sharing critical non-verbal information about each other.

Your first task is to decide when and where a hug or a handshake is the more appropriate gesture for you. This dilemma is not as simple to resolve as it may sound. There are two things to consider when making this decision. The first is whether you are someone who feels more comfortable with a simple handshake versus a hug. The second relates to the social situation in which you find yourself. Both are important, as the first human touch you have with a person will usually be through one of these mediums and it will reveal much about you and vice versa.

It is important in my opinion to, above all, be yourself. If you feel uncomfortable in general with hugs, other than with close family members, then a handshake might be the better option for you. If you are a natural hugger, then you might prefer a hug or a combination of a hug and a handshake, or a hug and a pat on the back. The key is to do whichever feels more comfortable for you. Always remember that the social brain of the other person will rapidly sense any falseness or discomfort if you go against your natural instincts.

Even if you are a hugger, you must be mindful of the social circumstances in which you find yourself. If it is a first meeting with someone say socially or professionally, it is often more appropriate to begin with a handshake. This allows both parties time to get to know the other. The conversation, if it went very well, might on occasion finish with a brief hug, but it is usually preferable if it begins with a handshake. During subsequent meetings, a brief hug or a combination of handshake and hug might feel more comfortable and appropriate for both parties, who may now feel more at ease with one another. In some cultures, a hug may be associated with a kiss on both cheeks or some air kissing. If this is felt to be comfortable by both parties, then this too may work for you.

It is essential to realize that touch, either as a hug or a handshake, as a form of non-verbal communication, must never be considered in isolation. If you can combine a hug or a handshake with a warm, welcoming open smile, good eye contact and good body language, you have already made an immediate, positive impression on the other person's social brain, without ever saying a word.

It is difficult to practise how we hug, as this is such an individual form of touch.

It is probably more important to practise when and how to use this form of touch in social situations and I encourage you to experiment with this in your everyday lives. There is little doubt that a genuine hug in the correct setting is one of the most powerful non-verbal forms of communication, often totally overriding the necessity for any words. But this has to feel both comfortable and genuine in nature. If you do not feel comfortable with this form of touch, then it is best avoided. Each person must decide whether or not this form of communication is for them.

As the handshake, however, is the more universal form of greeting with which most of us feel comfortable, we are going to focus principally on that.

Non-verbal Cues: Exercise Four

For one week, consciously pay attention to social interaction in situations involving handshakes, whether these occur at the beginning or towards the end of a conversation. There are two aspects to this exercise. The first relates to focusing on your own handshake. The second relates to information you can glean about the other person from the same handshake.

Let's begin with your own part in the handshake. There are some simple rules that you should practise during each introduction. Your palm should be straight, which is an open gesture. The grip pressure should be firm but not crushing. Above all, ensure that your grip is never limp, sweaty or weak in pressure. You should try to keep the handshake reasonably short, usually two to five seconds, as after this, the other person may feel uncomfortable.

Always make good eye contact with the other person at the same time and if possible greet them with a gentle smile, unless the situation is extremely formal or there is some other reason for keeping one's facial expressions neutral or subdued. Never try to pull the person into a closer embrace, during a first meeting in particular, as they may feel this is inappropriate. On finishing the conversation, it might feel appropriate or not to repeat a handshake. Try to be observant of which feels more comfortable at that moment in time.

You can also consciously learn much from how the other person in a social situation shakes hands with you. If the person's handshake is weak, limp or dead, this may tell you a lot about them. If they do not combine shaking hands with making good eye contact, this might suggest they are shy, anxious or not particularly interested in the interaction. If their grip pressure is too strong or they hold on too long to your hand, this too reveals a lot, as they may be trying to dominate you from the beginning. Your inner social brain will be picking up on these cues, but it is useful to focus on them consciously. This can help ensure that you are not making similar mistakes yourself, while recognizing their importance in forming an opinion about the other person.

You will be amazed at how quickly this exercise will help you to improve your handshaking skills in all kinds of social and working environments and how comfortable you will feel over time with this essential non-verbal cue. It will also amaze you how much information you can glean about those with whom you are networking.

Skill Five: How to Identify and Respect Personal Space

In the previous chapter we spoke about the importance of personal space and how the study of proxemics has given us some solid information as to what distances are appropriate and comfortable to adopt in social interactions. Personal space is a non-verbal form of communication in itself. It will say a lot about you for example if you are careful to respect other people's personal space when networking with them. While we may acknowledge this in theory, it is only through conscious awareness of personal space and practising your proxemic distances that you can unconsciously absorb this cue into your everyday communications. It is really all about being both mindful and respectful during these interactions. The following exercise will allow you to do just that.

Non-verbal Cues: Exercise Five

For one week, consciously focus during every social interaction on maintaining the correct interpersonal distance for that conversation. Because the vast majority of such interactions will occur within four to six feet, it is well worth focusing on these in particular. It is an interesting experiment to measure out this distance at home with a tape first. Notice for example how far you would have to stand from a wall or family member to achieve it. Measure the length of your arm and you will observe that maintaining approximately twice that length is a good rule of thumb to apply. Then in routine social interactions, consciously practise maintaining this proxemic distance. Try to be extremely conscious all the time of not invading the other person's space by getting any closer than four feet. Notice how uncomfortable you will feel if they inadvertently invade your space and, if this does happen, how you will instinctively back away. You will also begin to feel uncomfortable yourself if you inadvertently get too close to them. After a while you will unconsciously adopt this personal space distance for all social interactions.

For more personal interactions it is usually a lot easier and more comfortable to adopt space distances of one and a half to four feet. It is still useful to also measure out this distance to get a sense of what it looks like in practice, and then try to maintain this distance during such conversations. Practising this distance is important, as invading the space of someone you know reasonably well may also send out all the wrong non-verbal cues. Few of us will have any difficulties with intimate distance spacing, so spend most of your time on social and personal proxemic distances, until they become second nature.

It is also useful as part of this exercise to observe other people interacting and note how one or other party reacts if their personal space is invaded, even though this is usually completely unintentional. This will teach you to focus more on getting your own non-verbal cues right by guarding both your own and others' personal space.

Before we leave this section on non-verbal communication, let's see what happens to Graham when he decides to develop his connection skills in this area.

Graham's Story

Graham, in his late twenties and living with Margaret for several years, is really struggling at work and in his personal relationship. He comes from a high-achieving family and has learned from an early age that academic brilliance is what is expected of him. His father, a renowned academic, was a remote figure in his childhood who ruthlessly stamped out any display of emotions from his children. From an early age therefore, Graham has learned how to hide his emotions, keep his face impassive and avoid eye contact with others. He also avoids any form of tactile expressions in the form of hugs or handshakes, preferring a simple nod instead. Empathy is another casualty, as his mother is equally cold and non-emotional. In this, she takes after her father, so there is a pattern unfolding, one that would threaten to engulf Graham.

He was an excellent student and, following a brilliant academic career in computer engineering and software, is snapped up by one of the major tech companies. He quickly rises to managerial level, where his problems really begin. For starters, he works longer hours and starts to bring work home with him. His relationship with Margaret begins to suffer, not helped by his non-emotional reactions to the many concerns that she brings up. Sometimes, she protests, talking to Graham is like having a conversation with a robot. He seems cold, aloof, refuses to make eye contact and even on occasion avoids hugs and embraces. Her biggest obstacle, however, is a seeming disconnect between what Graham says verbally (which often seems sensible and rational) and his body language. She is becoming increasingly distressed, even considering whether it would be better to end the relationship, despite really loving the guy. She has met his family and understands why he is behaving the way he does, but this is not making it easier for her to live with him. As she admits to her mum, a warm and empathetic person, 'I love him to bits, but don't know if I can live with him for much longer.'

Meanwhile, at work, matters are also deteriorating. Graham has become manager of a new exciting team, who are young, eager, enthusiastic and full of ideas on how their section could progress further. His bosses are expecting great things from this dynamic team. Soon, however, tensions mount between Graham and his team members. No matter what exciting ideas or initiatives they bring to him, they receive little positive feedback or emotional response. He rationally explores the issues with them and verbally seems to be encouraging, but his whole body language screams the opposite. He seems uninterested, impassive, rarely showing any form of emotion or real support.

Clients too, find him hard to warm to and this shows in their responses to his team's advances. His own bosses are becoming increasingly frustrated with his overall performance levels and with the feedback from his team members (many of whom are female) that Graham is hard to work with. He is seen increasingly as non-empathetic, with some team members seeking transfers to other sections as a consequence.

Matters come to a head and Graham is called in for a perform-ance review, where many of these issues are highlighted. Gentle suggestions that his further role in the company might be under threat are made. He is given three months to turn things round. Margaret, meanwhile, has come to a decision that maybe it's time to take a break in their relationship and moves home for a month to review matters. Graham's life is going slowly downhill.

For once in his life, Graham decides to seek out some advice from a work colleague, who has the courage to tell him how it is. Why he is struggling with his work team, colleagues, clients and, especially, in his personal relationship. It is all about how Graham is coming across emotionally to others. It is not what he is saying verbally, but his complete lack of those soft but critical, non-verbal skills, that is creating his difficulties. He suggests that Graham visit a life coach, Martin, whom he himself has worked with in the past, and who has taught him a lot about this area. Graham attends a session with Martin and from this moment on, his life changes.

Following a long and detailed conversation, where Graham lays out his current difficulties, revealing in the process how his upbringing has shaped who he is today, it becomes increasingly clear to Martin that Graham's issues lie in his lack of non-verbal communication skills.

Martin then introduces him to the whole concept of emotional connection, and they begin by doing an inventory of his various skills in this area. It turns out for example that Graham is actually quite a good listener from a rational perspective, but often fails to pick up on the emotional aspects of a conversation. They also note some difficulties with his conversational style. Martin lays out some exercises to improve his techniques in these areas (some of which we have dealt with in earlier chapters). His primary difficulties, however, lie in his absence of normal routine non-verbal expressions. His lack of facial expression and his avoidance of eye contact during conversations. His tendency to avoid any form of tactile contact, even when deemed appropriate. His extremely poor body language in terms of posture and hand movements. The fact that there is no warmth in those rare moments when he does smile. And, most of all, that he is not allowing the world of emotions to be expressed through all of the above.

As Martin explains, all of these unconscious behaviours are making Graham seem cold and aloof, even though deep down this is not his intention. They agree that it is a consequence of his upbringing. Clearly, as Martin shares with him, they have much work to do!

Over the next few weeks, they tackle many of the problem areas highlighted, with Graham beginning to put them into practice in relation to his current working life and personal relationship. Thankfully, tensions in relation to the latter ease, as Graham reveals that he is now seeing Martin and promises that he will be working hard to put right many of the problem areas that they have uncovered. Margaret is delighted to see Graham tackle his issues and is now on board to assist him in achieving these new goals.

Martin and Graham begin by doing a joint video where the former interviews the latter, simulating a routine work conversation. This turns out to be a major surprise for Graham, who is quite dumbfounded on observing many of his mannerisms for the first time, most of which he had been unaware of. How blank his facial expressions are. How little eye contact he makes. How his body posture and hand movements seem so out of step with what he is discussing. Most of all, how unemotional and robot-like he seems. Throw in his natural aversion to touch, and he can now understand why Margaret for example is struggling with him emotionally. He is ready to begin whatever exercises Martin feels appropriate to right some of these issues.

They begin with some work on his facial expressions and eye contact. They discuss the importance of facial expressions in expressing how we feel emotionally about issues arising during routine conversations. Because Graham has been unconsciously shutting such expressions down for much of his life to date, it will require some significant conscious focus over the weeks to follow to improve his skills in this area. Over time, with a combination of both video work and focusing on every individual working and social interaction, Graham finds his facial expressions gradually beginning to mirror the emotions he is feeling at that moment in time. His face becomes increasingly expressive and he becomes increasingly aware of the positive impact this is having on others with whom he is conversing.

In parallel, he also begins to work on improving his eye contact. He finds this to be especially challenging, as his natural tendency is to either avoid eye contact completely or else to quickly look away from people with whom he is communicating. Martin teaches him the importance of making eye contact at the beginning of a social interaction and how to focus on the triangle between the eyes and nose and how to naturally switch contact regularly when chatting to someone. Once again, he practises this during routine social interactions until it becomes comfortable.

Martin also teaches him to smile more where appropriate, and to allow such a smile to reach his eyes. This turns out to be the single most important non-verbal cue he learns. It is a game-changer in both his personal and working life. As Graham learns increasingly over the weeks and months to follow, a warm genuine smile seems to short-circuit many working and social difficulties that might otherwise have arisen. It will become one of his most useful networking skills.

Two weeks later Martin takes a further short interactional video so Graham can see how he is progressing. He can barely recognize the person on the video in terms of facial expressions and eye contact. Gone is the lifeless look and the blankness. In its place is a normal human face that allows the emotions he was feeling to express themselves in a completely natural manner. He no longer has to think about it. It just occurs automatically. With Martin's assistance, he is now putting what he has learned into practice, in his everyday life. He uses every social interaction to practise his facial expressions, eye contact and smile. He notices how others are immediately warming more to him. It is doing no harm to his relationship with Margaret either, as it begins to blossom.

They then proceed to focus more on his body language and his aversion to touch. They begin with his body language, posture and hand movements. Once again, on reviewing their first video, Martin is able to point out some of his flaws in relation to all three. How regularly he tends to fold his arms in front of him, something he often does at work. How often he leans back in his chair and looks away from the person he is conversing with, which makes him seem bored or uninterested. How little he uses his hands at all. How often, when Martin asks him to continue the conversation standing up, he automatically puts his hands on his hips, suggesting once again, erroneously, that he wishes to dominate the other person. He can once again see how others might be picking up all the wrong messages, despite what he is verbally telling them.

Martin proceeds to show him what would present a more open image from a body-language perspective. This involves some simple changes such as never crossing his arms, leaning towards a person rather than away, never tilting his head away from them, sitting down in a more relaxed manner, never putting his hands on his hips, keeping his hands open rather than clenched, how to use his hands more effectively to express something emotionally, and many similar tips.

Graham then proceeds to put all of the information obtained from this video analysis into practice in his everyday communications, both at work and socially. In the beginning it feels strange and contrived. After a while, however, it becomes increasingly natural and automatic. These changes, allied to his improvements in facial expression and eye contact, are noticed at work by both colleagues and his bosses, who can see the positive effects they are having on his team.

The last link in the chain for Graham is to tackle his lifelong aversion to touch, which has come from his austere upbringing. He doesn't really like to be touched by others and even Margaret struggles with his difficulties in this area. He also dislikes handshakes, so pulls out of them quite quickly. This often comes across as a sign that he is not that trustworthy, which is not the case. He simply dislikes touch. He shies away especially from any form of hug or gentle embrace, from colleagues or socially. This makes him seem cold and distant, which is not assisting him in either domain.

On discussion, they decide that Graham is definitely more of a handshake rather than an embrace kind of guy. He could manage the former, but feels uncomfortable with the latter. He also agrees that a nod is simply not going to cut it in many social situations. Martin suggests they work hard on improving his handshake techniques firstly and then briefly discuss what to do in the area of hugs. They also agree that while it is useful to recognize how his upbringing is the source of his current issues with touch, this is not going to assist him much in terms of dealing with his current difficulties.

With Martin's assistance, Graham then begins to practise the correct handshaking techniques. He learns to keep his palm straight, grip pressure firm but not crushing, to maintain the handshake for two to five seconds and to make eye contact at the same time. He then begins to use this technique in his everyday social networking situations, until it becomes second nature and both comfortable and automatic. He also learns that there will be occasions where a short hug or gentle embrace is the mode of expression of the person whom he is meeting up with and that it is inappropriate to shy away from such interactions. He begins to put this into practice and finds to his surprise that after a while, this too becomes easier.

Within months, Graham's situation, as a result of all of his hard work, is completely transformed. His relationship with Margaret is now better than ever. But it is at work that the real benefits begin to accrue. He is now interacting with each member of his team on a personal basis. They are seeing him as increasingly human, someone they now feel comfortable opening up to about any issues that arise. Clients too are seeing the real person emerging from the shadows, and like what they are seeing. His team begins to flourish and grow, and others want to join it. His bosses are especially pleased, and bonuses and further advancement are also now being increasingly discussed.

There are so many messages emanating from Graham's story. How we are not trapped by the nature of our upbringing, but that we can change. How important non-verbal cues are, irrespective of how brilliant professionally or academically we are. How people warm quickly to those whose cues are open and friendly, and shy away from those who are closed systems. How often we can be so unaware of negative mannerisms and behaviours that build up over time, yet, when made aware of them and open to change, how rapidly we can undo them. How exercises and techniques, allied to use of videos, can be of enormous benefit in making such changes. Above all, how some simple hard work and dedication in the area of non-verbal communication can transform your whole emotional connecting world.

PART FOUR

WEEK 3:

HOW DO I INTERACT

WITH OTHERS?

9. People-To-People Communication Skills

In this section we are going to explore the more subtle aspects of good emotional connection in the form of people-to-people interactions. It is important that you have firstly laid down solid foundations as discussed in the previous two sections. If you have failed to work on your listening skills, conversational style or non-verbal cues, you may find it challenging to work on your people-to-people communication skills. It is like trying to build a house on dodgy foundations, the structure doomed to eventually give way. We will assume in this section that you have worked on these foundations and are now ready to progress to your people-to-people skills. There are two critical domains of life where people-to-people skills are especially useful, namely relationships and the workplace. But what are these skills?

People-to-people skills include emotional and cognitive empathy, compassion, how we interpret non-verbal cues, and how to smooth over and manage difficult social interactions. We can see immediately that these will involve us acquiring extremely subtle skills and techniques that elevate us into a different emotional connection stratosphere. Those who lack such skills will often find life, work and social interactions constantly fraught with difficulties. Those who have taken the time and effort to acquire these subtler skills, on the other hand, often find it easier to surf the turbulent waves of life.

The Interpretation of Non-verbal Cues

In the previous section we explored the world of non-verbal cues, but emotional connection involves more than simply being aware of such cues in ourselves and others. It also requires us to become more skilled during person-to-person encounters at interpreting such cues. This is more difficult than you might imagine.

It has happened to us all. We meet someone socially and experience an immediate 'gut' feeling of liking or disliking them. It is often not just about what they say verbally, but about the non-verbal cues they are sending out. We then make resulting snap decisions to encourage or discourage further contact. We tend to lock this information into our emotional memory and behave accordingly if we encounter them in the future. Later we discover that our assumption that a particular person is cocky, shy or rather aloof turns out to be false, as future interactions disclose the 'real' person.

But why does this happen? Why do we so often get it wrong in relation to reading such cues? The answer lies in your social brain, which as we explored in chapter two is set up to make lightning-fast subtle unconscious assessments of people whom you meet for the first time. This is a built-in safety mechanism to ensure that you can withdraw quickly from a social interaction if non-verbal cues seem unfavourable.

What such first impressions fail to reveal, however, are the myriad reasons a person may be giving off false cues as to how they are really feeling. It is not that the non-verbal cues emanating from the person are necessarily incorrect, it is more about interpreting what they mean. This is where it becomes important not to allow such impressions to dictate how we network with this person in the future.

Suppose you are coming through the duty-free shop at an airport and it is late at night. You encounter a lady at the till, who gives off all of the wrong non-verbal cues. Her facial expressions are blank, eyes fail to meet yours, body posture seems uninterested. You make an instant interpretation that this person is not very likeable, even a little surly, and you find yourself behaving accordingly.

You mention your feelings to your partner. They however have seen something completely different in the situation. 'Did you notice that that poor lady was completely exhausted,' they comment, 'she must have had a long day and is clearly at the end of her tether.' What has happened in practice is that they were less caught up in the moment of the interaction, instead mindfully or consciously assessing the greater picture.

What this little cameo demonstrates is the importance of not only noticing non-verbal cues during an interaction, but also interpreting them correctly. This will usually involve trying to make yourself consciously aware of the surroundings and circumstances surrounding the interaction. It will also involve holding fire on assuming that your first impressions of the person are correct. This is where the art of reading non-verbal cues comes into play.

This tendency to misread or misinterpret these cues is important in relationships and the workplace but is also important in how we respond to those suffering from mental health challenges. One of the commonest and most distressing difficulties that can arise for those undergoing a bout of clinical depression, for example, involves the misreading of non-verbal cues. This occurs in two ways. The person with depression struggles with reading the signs, focusing only on non-verbal cues that support their view that they are not worth being around. People who interact with them, on the other hand, also incorrectly misreading the cues, assume they are aloof, rude, boring or lazy.

This is also common in some forms of anxiety. Many people with social anxiety persistently misinterpret non-verbal social cues. They believe for example that the physical symptoms of anxiety will be noticed by others around them, which is untrue. They can also misread the facial expressions of those with whom they interact, finding danger or rejection where neither exists.

The misreading of non-verbal cues is one of the main signs of autism, and of what was previously known as Asperger's syndrome, which is now regarded as a condition on the autism spectrum. It explains why such conditions are so distressing for the sufferers. They can struggle to pick up on non-verbal cues and thus do not know how to respond to other people's emotions.

Later, we will be suggesting some exercises to assist you to become more skilled in this important person-to-person skill. These might save you from some embarrassing moments, as you later realize that your first impressions were, in retrospect, completely incorrect.

Empathy

Empathy is the ability to sense where another person 'is at' emotionally. It is the ultimate people-to-people skill. We all possess, but often fail to recognize, this innate ability. I often describe empathy as the capacity to open the door into the mind, heart and soul of another human being and vice versa. There are so many treasures to be found within every human being, so many mysteries to be unlocked. Empathy is the key that opens the lock to this door.

This ability to sense what is going on in the emotional world of another is facilitated by the mirror neuron system in the brain, which we discussed in chapter two. This allows our social and emotional brain to literally mirror what is going on in the mind and brain of the person we are interacting with. This is why we can on occasion become emotionally affected by what they reveal to us during a conversation. You too can learn to use this amazing internal system, to better effect this skill in yourself.

Empathy is the shortcut to you becoming a truly skilled emotional connector. It incorporates many of the skills already discussed, in particular listening and non-verbal cues. You may question the wisdom of including empathy as a skill at all. Is this not something we are born with, a natural capacity to relate to other human beings? Are not some fortunate in inheriting this capacity to a greater degree than others? Are they not the healers, doctors, spiritual leaders, teachers, nurses or therapists? And indeed, some people who are attracted to such vocations have the ability in abundance.

While some of these observations may be true, they overlook the amazing capacity of the human mind and brain, as discussed earlier, to learn and develop new skills. What a powerful message of hope, that you too can add empathy to your list of communication skills and in the process greatly transform your future life.

Empathy can be positive or negative. Our emotional brain can pick up positive or negative waves from another person and respond accordingly. Let's take a simple example. Today you pop into your local retail outlet. You meet a lovely woman, Deirdre, at the checkout. She engages with you in a friendly manner, assists you in packing your groceries and wishes you the best for the day.

You come away with a lighter step, a smile on your face. What a lovely interaction that was. You have just had a positive empathy experience!

The following week you pop into the same supermarket. You meet her opposite, Linda, at the checkout. She has a scowl on her face, refuses to assist you to pack your groceries, fires the change at you and ignores you as you leave. You come away with a heavier step and a frown on your face. What an unpleasant encounter that was. You have just experienced a negative empathy experience. Welcome to the world of empathy!

When most people think of empathy, they are automatically assuming that it is purely describing the creation of an emotional bond with another person with whom you are communicating, at that moment in time. With modern research we now understand that empathy has several strings to its bow. The modern view supported by many years of psychological and neuroscientific research is that empathy can be subdivided into three different but interlinking types.

Emotional Empathy

This is the most visceral form, where we unconsciously and automatically 'tune in' to another person's emotional state and often mirror their behaviour as a result. Although emotional empathy is normally an unconscious process, we can direct our conscious mind to it by becoming more self-aware of it in ourselves and others. This understanding will be critical when we explore the exercises in the next chapter, which will increase our awareness of this form of empathy.

I have always believed that positive emotional empathy must be the bedrock on which we build really strong, vibrant social connections with each other. But positive empathy bonds, essential in themselves, are regularly insufficient to assist those in difficult situations. There is also a significant risk that if we only focus on emotional empathy, we might burn out quite quickly. This is because during such empathy experiences and interactions, we are using up significant emotional reserves. This is the basis of compassion fatigue, so innate to those working in the medical, nursing and psychotherapy fields in particular.

Cognitive Empathy

This is where we have initially developed a positive emotional empathy bond with a person, but then progress to consciously identifying and understanding their feelings. For this reason it is often called 'perspective-taking'. This also frequently involves exploring more of the cognitive and behavioural aspects of these feelings or emotions or even becoming involved in a joint problem-solving cognitive interaction. Different parts of our brain are involved in cognitive versus emotional empathy, those more connected with problem-solving.

Cognitive empathy is seen as a more deliberate, thought-out process, and one therefore that is more open to being learned and practised as a skill. This is the form of empathy that allows doctors, nurses and therapists to assist those in distress, while keeping their own responses in perspective. This suggests that cognitive empathy involves putting a little space between the person and how their emotions have affected you, and in practice this is the case. What is happening in such situations is that a positive emotional empathy bond has already been set up, so both parties are instinctively now trusting that the other understands where they are at from an emotional perspective. This allows a more practical perspective-taking approach to take shape and this can greatly increase the total empathy bond between them.

Be wary however of simply trying to adapt this form of empathy, without firstly creating the emotional bond. Otherwise you may seem cold and non-validating to the person you are trying to assist, even if doing so with the best of intentions.

Compassion

This is best described as empathy in action. We have picked up emotionally on someone's feelings, consciously tried to identify them and as a result find ourselves moved to do something to assist them. A simple example might be where we encounter somebody homeless and feel an initial emotional empathy bond, cognitively take perspective on where they are at, and then respond with some practical steps to assist them.

Good emotional and cognitive empathy skills will allow you to navigate your social world with greater ease. We spend our lives in the presence of others, whether at home, work or in leisure activities. Struggling to sense where people are at from an emotional point of view makes these social interactions more challenging. You may also lose out on potential life-enhancing riches garnered by strong positive empathy bonds. Lack of empathy skills can be damaging and explains why some of us may struggle to be sensitive to the feelings of others, often riding roughshod over them. If you become more empathetic, however, you will observe yourself becoming more tolerant and sensitive to the feelings of others, more fulfilled in your everyday life and able to resolve social and working relationship problems more easily. All hallmarks of a great emotional connector.

Managing Difficult Social Interactions

Life will throw up multiple occasions where specific social interactions become fraught and often extremely difficult to manage. One of the most prized people-to-people skills, therefore, is the ability to smooth over such interactions and, if possible, to bring them to a satisfactory conclusion for all concerned. Everyday life is replete with situations where this skill could prevent potential conflict. There is not a single person out there who would not benefit greatly from acquiring this particular skill. Life is difficult enough without wasting time and emotional energy through not having the necessary networking skills to surf these awkward social minefields.

Those who have developed this skill are much better at managing work situations that are becoming toxic or at calming down relationship issues, whether to do with family, loved ones, friends, or within the community.

But why are such social interactions so challenging? It is important to answer this question if we hope to surf the waves of such encounters. Let's explore some of the challenges such interactions throw up.

1. It is an instinctive human response when challenged during such interactions to allow our emotions to take over and to make the issue personal. In such situations we tend to see the other person as attacking us, and as a response become emotionally heated. This of course makes the difficult social interaction even more challenging. We should instead be removing emotions from the picture and focusing more on the issues being brought up.

2. Sometimes we are not listening properly, focusing instead perhaps on trying to convince the other person of our point of view.

3. We take ourselves too seriously during such times and also see the interaction as a competitive situation that we have to win.

4. The biggest error is to fail to put ourselves empathetically in the other person's mind and try to see why this issue is so important to them. This will allow us to validate their emotions but also to shift the conversation into a more cognitive, problem-solving mode.

5. We may fail to let our non-verbal cues suggest that we are genuinely interested in working with the other person to sort out the issues involved. Remember, their social brain is scanning for cues to confirm or deny the validity of what you are saying to them.

6. We also may fail to sense that there is too much emotion being expressed at that particular moment in time. Or that it might be better on occasion to calmly bring the conversation to a close, with the promise that you will contact them as soon as possible, when you have had a chance to explore the issues being brought up.

7. Sometimes we may wish to bring up some difficult issues ourselves and find such interactions extremely distressing. This is because we are afraid of how the other person will respond emotionally and behaviourally. Will they get angry or annoyed? Will they storm off? Will it lead to prolonged periods of confrontation?

When one explores the above list of challenges, it becomes clear that to surf such difficult conversations will require superior people-to-people skills, often an amalgamation of all of those already discussed. In the next chapter we will explore how best to achieve the objective of being able to manage such interactions.

10. How to Improve Your
People-To-People Communication Skills

As explored in the previous chapter, people-to-people skills are the summit of emotional networking. It can be best described as connection in practice. But how do we develop such skills? In this chapter we will be suggesting some useful techniques to assist you in acquiring these most prized of all networking skills.

Skill One: How to Improve Your Empathy Skills

In the last chapter we discussed the importance of emotional and cognitive empathy. Not all of us however are especially skilled in these areas. You may for example really struggle with this skill and wonder how you can ever acquire it. I would like to reassure you that with a little bit of hard work and perseverance, you can transform your empathy skills. I strongly suggest the following exercises to achieve this objective.

People-To-People Observational Exercise
You cannot improve your emotional empathy skills unless you observe them in practice during everyday life. I recommend this observational awareness exercise for three days. **Focus fully**

on becoming consciously or mindfully aware of positive and negative empathy experiences in yourself and others. Open your mind to what happens at home, work, school, college and during leisure activities, when you or someone within your orbit reacts positively or negatively to whatever someone else is saying or doing.

It could be observing what happens when a child or a teenager asks their parent a question. If the parent responds empathetically, you will observe the positive response of the child. If the parent's response is negative, observe the reactions of the child. It could be at work when a colleague, or indeed yourself, receives a positive or dismissive response to some observation or request made of a work colleague or boss. Once again, you may notice hackles rising if experiencing a negative empathy experience and vice versa if positive. It could occur within your relationship, or when engaging in a sporting activity, or when involved in any interaction with friends or others. You may observe someone, depending on the empathy interaction experienced, responding positively or pulling back. It may occur during an interaction involving a service, whether shopping, banking or attending the dentist, doctor or nurse. Become aware of how you are responding and how other people are responding to you.

You will quickly notice that you are becoming increasingly observant of social interactions you had previously taken for granted, and increasingly aware of the positive or negative effects of your own interactions with people and how you are more tuned in to them emotionally. You will have developed a 'radar' for positive and negative empathy, noticing how you and others respond behaviourally to both.

People-To-People Skills: Exercise One

Now that you have made yourself consciously aware of the importance of emotional empathy within the social world you inhabit, it is time to begin practising this skill yourself. **For one week, every time you engage with somebody within your social world, focus only on the person you are communicating with. In each interaction, as you had to do during the listening and conversing exercises, consciously and mindfully push yourself into the background.** This is much harder to put into practice than you might think. We are all a bit self-obsessed, only interested in what pertains to our own little world.

With this exercise, the whole focus should be on trying to sense emotionally where the person is at. Involve yourself emotionally in the story they are telling you, at that moment in time. Are they sad, happy, hurt, annoyed or frustrated? Feel yourself being drawn into where they are at. It requires patience and sometimes intense concentration when performing this exercise the first few times. Your instinct may be to rush in and move the interaction to where you would like it to go. This may end up with you missing the emotional impact of the conversation topic on the person you are interacting with.

If you are performing this exercise fully, you will begin to observe your own emotions mirroring those of the other person. You may feel sad or joyful while interacting with their experiences. This is the first real sign that you are opening the door into their hearts and minds. This is the point where you can begin to share your own experiences and emotions about what has been discussed. For, now, you are experiencing a two-way meeting of minds. From this point on, it is like singing from the same hymn sheet emotionally. You will notice that both parties enjoy leaving the conversation with a positive empathy experience.

Over time and with practice, you will observe how you are listening with your whole body, not just your ears. Your emotional brain is tuning in to the music emanating from the other person's emotional world. You will observe yourself speaking less, listening more and responding instinctively to the other person, as they reveal something especially difficult or sad. This you will begin to do automatically, almost without thinking, as your two worlds meet and share the experience.

When you notice yourself being gentler, warmer and more careful with other people's emotions, you have truly arrived. You will discover a richness in others' emotional experiences that you might have spent your life missing out on.

If you practise this exercise constantly, the benefits will remain with you for life, for this is a skill that, once developed and practised, you can automatically and unconsciously apply for life. You will sense people being more comfortable around you, often revealing core insights that otherwise would have remained hidden. Your life will consequently be enriched. When difficulties arise in life, you will handle them better, as emotional empathy skills will significantly ease the journey.

It is also important during this week to develop your cognitive empathy side, so every time you engage with somebody within your social or working world, having created an emotional empathy bond with them, consciously focus, where appropriate, on progressing to creating a cognitive empathy bond. This will mean that you work together with them, where appropriate, to take a perspective on issues that may have arisen. It may mean that you merge your two minds together, into a joint problem-solving mode, if they seek your assistance with some issue or difficulty they are encountering. There will be some social interactions where clearly this will not be necessary and the emotional empathy bond created during the conversation will be sufficient. In such situations, there is no need to progress any further.

But there will be many situations where the other person may be extremely interested, even grateful for your assistance, in gaining a new or different perspective on something troubling them. They are already comfortable, as you have created an emotional empathy bond, so trust your judgement when you share your perspective on the issue in question with them. This will often lead to a back-and-forth cognitive empathy experience, which will enrich both people.

At other times, they might be grateful for your input into some major problem or life difficulty that they are experiencing at the time, whether in relation to work, relationship, family, finances or anything else. This also requires that an atmosphere of trust has already been created through emotional empathy. In these situations, the creative, problem-solving part of your brain begins to mirror, almost like a series of computers linked together. The results of this chain reaction can be powerful indeed, with solutions to problems previously felt to be insolvable emerging.

In the beginning, this exercise will seem strange and require once again an enormous amount of mindful concentration, but gradually you will find yourself becoming more skilled in knowing when and how to progress into these cognitive empathy areas. The emotional connection benefits that will subsequently accrue will be major indeed. If you can assist someone in difficulty with this mixture of emotional and cognitive empathy, you will have a friend for life.

These powerful exercises will gradually assist you to integrate empathy into your everyday life. Bit by bit, through constant practice and repetition of these techniques, you will notice how your people-to-people empathy communication skills are rapidly becoming more effective.

Skill Two: How to Interpret Non-verbal Cues

It is one thing to become aware of the importance of non-verbal cues, but quite another to become aware of their presence and know how to interpret them more effectively, in routine people-to-people social networking situations. Hopefully the following exercise will assist you to develop your skills in this area.

People-To-People Skills: Exercise Two

As already discussed, when chatting to someone, we are unconsciously absorbing non-verbal messages. It is a fascinating exercise, however, to consciously focus our rational or logical mind on interpreting non-verbal cues emanating from the other person. **For one week, consciously focus on the non-verbal information coming from other people during every social interaction.** You will need to remove your natural inclination to focus on yourself during each conversation for this to be effective. Become mindfully aware of the person's facial expressions, eye contact, tone of voice, bodily stance or posture, how they use their hands, the presence or absence of muscle tension, and any other relevant information. We have already discussed these cues in the previous two chapters.

Now assess if these non-verbal cues seem at one, or out of character, with what the person is saying. For example, a person might be expressing sorrow about something, while non-verbal cues suggest otherwise. Or they may be laughing at some joke, while their body language or facial expression indicates they are not amused. When you leave the social interaction in question, review, either on paper or in your mind, what overall impressions you gained about the person in question. Was there an obvious lack of non-verbal cues? Did the person come across as being genuine to you? Did their non-verbal cues set off any warning signals? Did you sense that you were not being given the whole story in a situation, despite the words being spoken?

This is a powerful exercise, assisting you to become increasingly aware of non-verbal cues emanating from others and how to interpret what they are implying. By consciously focusing on such non-verbal cues over time, you will increasingly begin to do this automatically. You will also discover that your skills in this area rapidly improve and that you develop a sixth sense when something feels off.

We also discussed in previous chapters how quickly our social brains make lightning-fast assessments when meeting someone for the first time. How such social interactions lead to us forming first impressions of the person in question and how such impressions are difficult to shift once formed. How these impressions can be extremely valuable and sometimes accurate, but later are often found to be off-kilter.

If you are regularly putting your foot in it socially, and are constantly misreading cues and later feeling foolish, then during the same week, seek out non-verbal cues in every social situation, on your initial meeting with a person. List your first impressions in your notebook when you have a moment. Then, seek out evidence subsequently to prove or disprove whether these first impressions are accurate. This might mean seeking information from other sources as to what the person is like in real life. Or probing the person more deeply during subsequent meetings. In such situations, try to uncover evidence, supportive or not, of your first impressions. Or, when reflecting subsequently on the interaction, consider whether the non-verbal cues clashed with what the person was saying. That might lead you to question why this might be.

You will be amazed how often first impressions are false. This occurs because, as previously discussed, the social brain has learned to make lightning-fast observations and conclusions in such situations. It then leaves it up to your rational brain to seek out evidence to the contrary. There are often reasons why a person's non-verbal cues are out of kilter. They may be anxious or depressed, or good at masking how they feel. They may be tired or worn out, or worrying about some major crisis going on in their lives. We may not be getting a true picture of the person at all. Some of us are very deep and, like a sculptor, you may have to chisel away at the surface to discover what lies beneath.

There will be occasions where you are certain that these first impressions are correct, others where you are unsure. Write down the results of these assessments in your notebook. In time, further evidence may appear that will strengthen or weaken these conclusions. You can later compare initial assessments with concluding ones. It can be a salutary, often humbling, experience to discover how inaccurate your first impressions were.

A good rule of thumb is to assume first impressions are frequently wrong and treat them with extreme caution until proven otherwise. This exercise will assist you in accepting that your reading of non-verbal cues emanating from others, while helpful, can on occasion be completely inaccurate. Learning to be patient and taking the effort to uncover confirmatory evidence can save you from a world of trouble!

Skill Three: How to Manage Difficult Social Interactions

We explored in the previous chapter the challenges involved in managing difficult social situations. This is a people-to-people skill that is extremely prized and is a sign to others that you have truly arrived as a skilled emotional connector. Navigating the minefields of such interactions, however, requires a lot of patience and personal insight. There will be many readers who would dearly love to acquire this skill and you may be one of them. Hopefully the following exercise will be of assistance.

People-To-People Skills: Exercise Three

For one week practise the following exercise. As any difficult interactions occur socially or at work, use those situations as an opportunity to improve your people-to-people skills by doing the following:

1. **Consciously practise remaining calm and quiet, no matter how much heat is being generated.** If necessary and if you are close to 'losing it', withdraw for five minutes perhaps to make a cup of coffee or visit the bathroom. When feeling calm, return to continue the conversation. A key thought in difficult social interactions should be that 'one should never throw petrol on a fire!' Calm sucks oxygen out of the inferno, ensuring that the fire goes out more quickly.

2. **Work on ensuring that you do not make the matters under discussion 'personal'** (it can be useful sometimes to state this). Focus consciously instead on returning continually to the problem, issue or difficulty under discussion and try to adopt a problem-solving approach.

3. **Consciously concentrate on listening carefully and empathetically to the other person's point of view and on validating their emotions and concerns.** Try to focus on why this issue is causing them so much emotional upset. Try to read between the lines as to what they may not be saying; or is there something that you are overlooking yourself? Is there something going on in the person's life that might be influencing their current upset? What are you picking up from their non-verbal cues?

4. Once you have done the above, it becomes easier to calmly bring the conversation under control and **see if a joint problem-solving exercise might resolve the issue involved**. Do not be afraid to suggest that you would like to take some time to consider their views and concerns and will come back to them later, to see if they could be addressed. This often takes further heat out of the situation, reassures the other person that you are truly listening to them and allows you some time and space to come up with some potential solutions.

5. There will be some situations where, despite your best intentions, the other person is simply not prepared to either listen or compromise. The important skill here is to **show that you have validated their concerns, remain calm and leave the door open to a potential further meeting** at a later date, when hopefully some of the emotional heat has been removed from the situation in question.

If you practise this exercise during this week and onwards, you will notice how quickly you automatically switch into this confrontation-management mode, when such encounters occur. The benefits to you socially and to your career will be immense.

Before departing this section, let's see what happens firstly to Ruth and then to Jill, when both decide, for personal and professional reasons, to develop their people-to-people communication skills.

Ruth's Story

Ruth's personal life is in turmoil as yet another romantic relationship bites the dust. As she admits to her best friend Gillian, she is simply terrible at reading guys and situations, and is constantly, as a result, making bad relationship decisions. In her late thirties, she feels time is running away from her and is becoming increasingly anxious, as she has always wanted to meet someone and have a family. Her personal life is in sharp contrast to the rest of her life, where, to date, she has been extremely successful. She has a high-powered job in the financial world where her great organizational skills have proved to be invaluable, and she is extremely popular with her colleagues.

Gillian, who by this stage is well versed in Ruth's romantic difficulties and who is happily ensconced in a long-term relationship herself, is empathetic to her plight. She suggests that, as this is the fifth relationship to have broken up over the previous two years, maybe it is time to change tack. She is brutally honest with her friend. 'You are going to have to get some assistance to learn how to read guys better, and become more adept at picking up on warning signs when something is off-kilter.' She suggests working with a therapist friend, Clara, who has assisted other friends and colleagues in these areas.

Ruth is sceptical but agrees to work with Clara. After a long chat with the therapist it becomes clear to both that Ruth is poor at picking up on and assessing non-verbal cues, often discovering later that her first impressions were incorrect. She also struggles when it comes to reading people in general, but men in particular, as her current personal relationship difficulties demonstrate.

On briefly reviewing her five previous unsuccessful relationships together, it is clear that her lack of skills in these areas led to each one collapsing in turn. There is a clear pattern emerging here and it relates to her people-to-people skills. Clara also picks up on other communication difficulties in relation to her listening and conversational styles and they do some work in these areas. They then progress to exploring her people-to-people skills. It is hard for Ruth, who has been so successful in all other areas of life, to accept that she is a novice when it comes to some of these skills. She is honest enough, however, to accept that she has work to do, and agrees to work with Clara to improve matters.

They begin with a discussion on the world of non-verbal cues, which Ruth finds fascinating. It is not something she has ever really considered when networking with others. Clara explores the importance of facial expressions, eye contact, tone of voice, body posture, hand gestures and the importance of personal space etc. in relation to everyday social interactions. She then gives Ruth an exercise where she is to spend the following week consciously focusing on these cues, during every social networking situation. She is also to assess whether these observed non-verbal cues seem out of place with what the person is verbally communicating at the time. Do the two seem to be in harmony? What does it mean if the person for example does not maintain eye contact or has a limp handshake? She is also to observe others in similar social conversations and assess their non-verbal cues.

Ruth finds the week of observing such cues extremely enlightening. For starters, it makes her increasingly aware of the importance of the signals she is sending out when conversing with others. It also greatly improves her conscious awareness of these cues in those she is interacting with. She begins to watch for little 'tells' that might indicate something is out of kilter during the interaction, and to take note of this for future reference.

Clara also asks Ruth, for the week in question, during every social interaction to list her first impressions of the person in a notebook. Then she is given the task of seeking out information from further sources or future meetings as to whether such impressions are accurate or not. Do their non-verbal cues for example match up? Does Ruth probe deeply enough during the initial interaction to be sure of her first impression? Does she discover later that the person in question struggles with anxiety or is under some other significant pressure? Does a subsequent meeting throw doubt on her original first impressions?

Ruth is astonished to note how often her first impressions turn out to be flawed – on occasion, significantly so. She is now feeling ashamed on reflecting on how many men she has rejected almost instantly throughout the previous five years, due to negative first impressions. She is also rueful when she thinks of the possible nice guys she may have missed out on. Clearly, she is going to have to change her approach.

Clara suggests that she adopts a new philosophy of assuming that her first impressions are wrong until proven otherwise when it comes to assessing others, especially men, in the future. They agree that sometimes women may form a particularly strong negative first impression of certain males, and that one must not immediately overrule this feeling. Neither should Ruth be foolish in such situations, but take the normal precautions. It is the normal routine impressions socially, however, that she is to take special heed of.

All of this information feeds in nicely to the next step, where Clara tries to assist Ruth to improve her general reading of people and in particular potential romantic partners. This will involve acquiring an overall global impression of someone, both initially and over a longer period of time. Ruth is now given the task of consciously focusing on trying to get a read on what she feels about the person she is interacting with in every working and social interaction. As Clara emphasises, this will require listening more than conversing, assessing them emotionally, getting a sense of their body language and non-verbal cues and trying to decide if they seem genuine or not. Do any of the above strike a warning bell, for example? Does something feel off-kilter? Do they come across as genuine and sincere or do their actions or non-verbal cues seem false or hollow over time? Do their intentions seem to be honourable or not? Do you sense that this is someone you trust? Over time, do your impressions remain the same, or do you notice that you are subtly altering them, as more information is gleaned?

Ruth finds this an extremely challenging exercise to carry out and is frequently exhausted in the beginning with the conscious effort required to maintain the necessary focus and concentration. Gradually, however, she begins to notice that her reading of people, whether known to her already or strangers, is rapidly improving. She is now noticing small things that hitherto she would have completely overlooked. She also learns to take her time in terms of reading people, as so much reveals itself in the process. She becomes increasingly comfortable with her overall impressions or reading of others, and it soon becomes something she does automatically. This will, in the future, turn out to be an extremely useful tool at work. For the present she is now ready to turn her attentions to personal relationships, with all of the information gleaned.

Over the months that follow and with Clara's encouragement, she re-enters the dating scene with a lot more confidence in her people-to-people skills. As Clara explains, successful personal relationships must have two key ingredients. The first is that 'buzz' or 'electricity' between both parties, which both women agree good-humouredly is essential. The second key is an open flowing communication between both parties. It is within this second area that Ruth will now have to apply all she has learned.

Her first task is to stop shutting out guys simply because her first impressions are negative, especially if there is a 'buzz'. This immediately increases the pool of potential candidates. Her next task is to begin, over time, to get a better overall read on those who seem more interesting. This proves to be a lot easier following on from the work she has done with Clara. She develops a sixth sense as to when something feels off and shuts down such relationships. She also feels herself becoming more comfortable in giving other relationships time to see if they could grow or flourish. In time, all of her hard work bears fruit. She meets Andy, with whom there is plenty of electricity, but who over time also reveals himself to be a warm empathetic guy, with whom she feels increasingly comfortable. Over the following nine months to a year, this relationship begins to deepen. As she admits to Gillian, all of her hard work is finally bearing fruit.

Jill's Story

Jill, who is in her forties and in an explosive long-term relationship with partner Percy, is in trouble again. She is renowned for having a short fuse and for her inflexibility in relation to dealing with difficult situations in both her social and working life. Not especially renowned for her empathy skills, she is however famous in her industry, for her business skills and know-how. This is the only reason she is still employed by her current company. But even their patience and forbearance is stretched as problems within her department mount up, with Personnel receiving complaint after complaint from frustrated colleagues struggling to deal with her.

At home, and within her wider family and friends, Jill is also struggling. Percy has threatened to leave on a number of occasions and intimates that he is close to taking that final step. Jill loves him dearly, so this information brings her up short, as she visualizes the empty life that would face her if Percy were to leave. Her close friends, even her sisters, have been on the receiving end of her behaviour on occasion and they too are pulling back.

Finally, after a significant client threatens to withdraw their account, following yet another argument with Jill on the phone, her company boss decides that action will have to be taken. Jill is given a final warning and only survives when she agrees to work with Personnel on improving her people-to-people skills. They suggest that she might work with Martin, a life coach, whom we met in previous chapters. Jill reluctantly agrees to work with him.

Martin turns out to be a warm, non-judgemental life coach, with whom Jill immediately bonds. She reveals her difficulties at work, home and with partner, family and friends. It becomes increasingly clear to Martin that many of her difficulties relate to a combination of a lack of emotional empathy and her inability to manage difficult networking interactions that are part and parcel of everyday life. Jill, who is brutally honest and rational in relation to both herself and others, agrees, and seeks Martin's assistance in trying to improve in these areas.

They begin with a long discussion about empathy, why it is so important in relation to our dealings with other people and the difference especially between emotional and cognitive empathy. They also discuss the difference between positive and negative empathy. This is like visiting a foreign country for Jill, for whom emotions or feelings have always been seen as weaknesses, to be quickly stamped out and replaced with cold hard factual reality. Martin explains that while the latter approach might work in some aspects of business, it usually ends up as a disaster in terms of our routine working and personal relationships. Lack of empathy also makes it more challenging to manage difficult social interactions.

On exploring her upbringing, Martin discovers that Jill's mum was an extremely successful businesswoman, who has instilled a belief in her daughter that expressing emotion is a sign of weakness, especially if one hoped to succeed as a woman in a man's world. Her father was the opposite, a warm, emotionally nuanced man, just like her brother. Alas, Jill has absorbed more of her mother's traits and as time has passed has learned to consolidate them further. This seems to lie at the heart of her current difficulties. Clearly Jill will have to work on her empathy skills if they are to proceed any further.

Jill is puzzled, as she has always assumed that empathy is an inherent trait, which some of us lack, while others have it in abundance. Martin explains that while there is some truth in this statement, it belies the fact that each one of us has an innate capacity to change, to develop and practise new skills, with empathy a simple example of this in practice. Even though Jill has absorbed some of her mother's negative messages in relation to empathy, it is within her power to change. She is heartened by this information and is now ready to work on her skills in this area.

Martin begins by giving Jill an emotional empathy awareness exercise, where she is to spend a number of days consciously observing positive and negative social interactions going on around her, whether at home, work or socially. This is a mind-boggling exercise for Jill, as she, for the first time in her life, stops and mindfully becomes aware of the effects of positive and negative empathy on others. How colleagues at work respond instantly to the former and shrink if exposed to the latter. How friends and family behave in a similar manner.

She even begins to notice it when customers in stores experience different empathy responses, and the reverse, the effects on the staff in such situations, when customers behave poorly or not. It is a real eye-opener and makes Jill ruefully reflect on her own actions and behaviours to date. She can now see why Percy and her work colleagues are struggling so much with her. Things clearly are going to have to change.

Martin then requests that for the following week and onwards Jill puts into practice what she has learned. He asks her to consciously focus on every social interaction, on trying to create an emotional empathy bond with the person with whom she is networking. This would involve specifically focusing on the emotions emanating from the person as they are telling Jill about something going on in their working or social life at that moment. He tells her she will find this difficult, as all of us are self-obsessed and more interested in our own feelings and stories. She will have to be both patient and able to pay absolute attention to the other person, if she is to be successful in this task.

Her objective is to try to internally sense where the other person is at emotionally, during each conversation. Are they feeling sad or happy or annoyed, for example? If she is doing this exercise correctly, she may even begin to feel the same emotions herself, something that up to this date would have seemed foreign to her. She might even feel herself mirroring what the other person is feeling. If this happens, she has arrived.

Jill really struggles with this exercise to begin with but, with Martin's encouragement and with perseverance, she senses that something is changing within her. She is beginning to feel closer to those she is interacting with, sensing more and more how they are feeling in different situations. She also notices how she is listening more and saying less. She comments to Martin how, instinctively, on a number of occasions, she has even found herself touching the other person on the arm or giving them a hug, if something really sad or emotional is being discussed. This for Jill is a major break-through, as she has previously shunned such emotional reactions.

The effects of these changes are already showing. The relation-ship between Percy and herself is deepening. Her colleagues at work are also noticing the changes and warming more to her by the day. Following some further work on her cognitive empathy skills, Martin is now ready to progress to assisting Jill in relation to her management of difficult or confrontational networking situations, both at work and within her personal relationship and wider family.

They discuss the issues that make such potential conflict situations so problematic. These include losing her cool too quickly, making matters personal rather than focusing on the problem in question, not showing empathy towards the other person, refusing to see their point of view, wanting others and the world to change, but not herself, amongst others.

To counteract such issues, Martin asks Jill to focus on a different strategy any time she finds herself in a potentially difficult social situation over the following week and onwards. This will involve, for starters, retreating for five minutes from the situation if she is struggling to keep her emotions in check. She finds this suggestion particularly useful and has to use it a lot for the first few weeks. As Martin comments, 'It's wiser not to throw petrol on a fire!' After a while she notices that she is bringing her emotions under control more rapidly, and is better able to avoid those trips to the bathroom!

Martin also suggests that she uses the information gained from her empathy exercises to sense where the other person is at emotionally, and this is quite an enlightening experience. He counsels her to constantly reassure the person in question that this is not personal, but that she is genuinely trying to resolve the issue in question. She finds this piece of advice especially useful.

Jill puts this advice into action over the weeks that follow, noting how quickly she can remove the heat from such situations, moving both parties instead to a problem-solving mode. She makes a special effort to ensure that the other person's views and feelings are validated, and learns to appreciate that there are many ways of looking at the same situation other than from her own perspective. This is a chastening experience. She also learns to use humour a lot more, to prevent such potential conflicts from ever getting off the ground.

Within months, Jill's working and personal life have been completely transformed as a consequence of all her hard work and dedication. At work her colleagues are no longer afraid to come to her with difficult issues, which before might have led to flare-ups. Now, she listens more attentively, is more empathetic, validates their position on issues brought up and is more focused on solving rather than highlighting problems. Clients, too, find her easier to network with and she soon becomes the person to go to, to resolve issues that hitherto might have led to conflict. At home, Percy and herself are no longer in constant conflict and the benefits that accrue to both are immense. There is still the odd flare-up, as would be the norm with all couples, but now there is a respect and a desire to prevent such potential conflicts from growing legs.

Jill is well on her way to becoming a truly skilled emotional connector.

These two stories demonstrate the importance of people-to-people skills in practice. How a lack of such skills can lead to so much emotional turmoil in our lives. How their presence, on the other hand, can transform our social world for the better. The key message being that any of us can develop such essential connection skills. All that is required is hard work and perseverance. Try it and see for yourself.

We are now ready to move into the final section, where we explore the personal skills that, if acquired, will put a final gloss on your emotional connection skills.

PART FIVE

WEEK 4:

AM I CONFIDENT ENOUGH?

11. Personal Development Skills

The final part of our journey involves self-awareness, or personal development skills. These are the really hidden, subtle skills, the true arbitrators of how effective or not your communications with others will be. You have already worked on some essential aspects of communication such as your listening and conversational techniques, non-verbal cues and person-to-person skills. There are, however, other hidden skills that you need to consciously focus on to become a polished emotional connector.

These personal development skills include the following:

1. Self-Acceptance. How to be comfortable in one's skin and treat ourselves and others as equals and with respect.
2. The importance of being yourself.
3. Humour and not taking oneself too seriously.
4. Kindness and compassion towards ourselves and others.
5. Gratitude.
6. Managing and banishing frustration and hurt from social interactions.

Let's explore these in greater detail.

Self-Acceptance

Have you ever had the experience of meeting someone who seems totally at ease with themselves, and envied their ability to be so comfortable in their own skin? How they as a result put you, too, completely at ease. These are the people who have developed unconditional self-acceptance and have learned to apply the same principle to others. These are also the people towards whom others instinctively gravitate. Social interactions with them never seem to be rushed and you often leave their presence feeling better about yourself and the world you find yourself residing in.

Why are such individuals so comfortable in their own skin? The answer lies in their conscious decision not to rate or judge themselves as a person, no matter the circumstances that arise. In other words, they are choosing not to become involved in the rating game, which is so destructive. In this game, each one of us rates or measures ourselves as a person positively or negatively, depending on how successful or not we are in relation to our actions, skills or talents. Maybe you too can see yourself falling into this trap. If for example you fail at a task, do you see yourself as a failure as a person? If successful, do you see yourself as a success? In other words, do you merge who you are as a person with the success or failure of your actions, skills or talents? This is of course a recipe for unhappiness.

The world of social media, and indeed modern life itself, lives and breathes the toxic atmosphere of self-rating. So many of our young people are caught up in this rating game, making them anxious, stressed and depressed.

Those who choose instead the road of unconditional self-acceptance will seem different when emotionally connecting with others. There are certain characteristics that you will notice in members of this group. They seem at ease with themselves and with life and also put those who interact with them at ease. They refuse to become personally upset or bothered if other people are seemingly rating them as a consequence of their actions, focusing instead on whether assessments of the latter seem accurate or appropriate or not.

They are also comfortable admitting to weaknesses or owning up to having made errors, accepting that they are not perfect but can only do their best in every situation. They are equally adept at refusing to rate or measure other people, seeing them too as human like themselves and prone to errors, weakness and failure. This means that they are non-judgemental and more forgiving of others and this comes across strongly in their social interactions. If we're honest, these are the people that seem easier to love and feel close to, and also those that we most want to emulate in life.

Why is self-acceptance so important for social communication? The answer lies in the manner in which those who practise it are making such interactions easier to navigate. When you encounter these powerful emotional connectors, you know that you will be treated with respect, will be listened to and validated, and that nothing you say or do will seem to shake the solid foundations on which these special individuals seem to be built. You can therefore be yourself in their presence. They will not judge you or take umbrage at any comment you might inadvertently make. You will be treated as an equal. You therefore relax and feel comfortable sharing information with them, sensing that they will treat you as they treat themselves, with dignity and acceptance. What a lovely experience to have.

One of the primary reasons that you may struggle to develop unconditional self-acceptance is your internal critical voice, called the 'pathological critic'. You may be familiar with this inner voice, constantly nagging and berating you for making even the smallest mistakes in your everyday life. This is the voice in your head, shaped by upbringing and events in your adult life, that tends to criticize you intensely if things are not going well. We all hear this voice, at times, with its snide comments suggesting you are 'useless', 'weak', 'a failure', 'worthless' or 'abnormal'. It is the pathological critic that drives our tendency to rate ourselves in this manner.

The pathological critic is, of course, your internal emotional mind. Normally the rational brain and mind attempt to control the emotional brain, with limited success. Imagine a so-called good friend who rings you daily, gleefully informing you of your shortcomings. Eventually you begin to believe that he must be telling the truth. Now visualize this friend ringing you incessantly throughout the day with these relentless, deprecatory comments. This is what it feels like when the pathological critic gets out of control.

To achieve unconditional self-acceptance, however, you will have to discover a method of taking on your pathological critic, otherwise you will always struggle with being comfortable in your own skin, something that will be obvious to others when networking. We will be exploring in the next chapter how to challenge this voice. Developing self-acceptance and learning how to bring it into emotional connection situations is not easy and will require some time and effort to acquire it. The benefits that you will accrue however are immense. For this is the ultimate personal connection skill, the real secret to becoming a great communicator. Later, we will explore how you too can achieve this.

The Importance of Being Yourself

After self-acceptance, one of the most important personal skills for effective emotional connection relates to being yourself in social interactions. How many of us struggle to do just that? Our social brains are well attuned, often unconsciously, to deciding whether someone with whom we are communicating seems authentic or not. Do they seem genuine and sincere or trying to be someone they are not? These attributes really matter to us as human beings, as they help us to build up trust with others. Yet we rarely focus on their importance in relation to everyday social interactions.

When communicating with another person, it is essential that they believe that you are sincere in relation to your thoughts, emotions and actions. This means that they sense that what you are expressing as feelings is backed up by non-verbal cues such as tone of voice, facial expressions and eye contact. If they sense that your expressed emotions are insincere, it is the death knell for everything else that follows in relation to that conversation and subsequent ones. You may be an excellent verbal communicator but if you fall down here, you will really struggle.

In a similar vein, most of us sense pretty quickly whether someone with whom we are communicating seems genuine or not. We are, in such situations, putting together a global impression as to whether the person is who they claim to be from an emotional and behavioural perspective. Once again, this really matters to us, even if only subliminally. We are more likely to connect better with, and trust more, those who seem to be genuine in nature. This global impression is gleaned from a composite picture gained from all of the attributes of emotional connection that we have already detailed. We sense whether others are good listeners, speak horse-sense, are in tune with their body language, comfortable with themselves and sincere.

Clearly all of us will get it wrong on occasion. We will encounter people who at first glance, and perhaps even subsequently, may seem sincere and genuine. But over time the mask slips and we see the real person emerging, often revealed through their subsequent behaviour. This can be upsetting, and we may feel really let down at such times.

If you work on these attributes, however, and remain true to yourself, you will ensure that you present an authentic, genuine and sincere image to others. You will also become more adept at picking up warning signs of their absence in others. All signs of a skilled communicator. We will be exploring how you can achieve this in the next chapter.

A Sense of Humour

The great networkers not only accept themselves unconditionally, but also understand the importance of humour in social interactions. Humour has many important strings to its bow. It can often take the heat out of a difficult situation. It can lighten the tone of a conversation, while still giving you the opportunity to get a point across. Humour also has the capacity to break through uncomfortable social interactions.

The secret of course is to have a profound sense of humour about both yourself and life. This has the added benefit of showing others that you are refusing to take yourself too seriously. It is so much easier to deal with someone who takes this stance than someone who takes the opposing one. How often for example have you met people in social situations who take themselves too seriously? Think how uncomfortable you feel in their presence.

How you feel that you are walking on eggshells while around them, even becoming guarded in your comments.

Clearly, humour for some of us comes easier than for others. Some of us are by nature more serious and find humour hard to come by. But it is a personal communication skill that all of us can improve on. All of us can work on 'lightening up' a little in terms of how we view ourselves. Those who become more skilled in this area will become more effective communicators. More on this later.

Kindness

We live in a brutal world, where kindness can be a rare commodity indeed. Life for many of us can be harsh, unforgiving and unyielding. When we encounter the gentle cloak of kindness, it can come sometimes as a real shock to our system. Those who work on being kind to themselves and to others will find this tendency greatly assists them in their social networking. Kindness will often involve both accepting the other person where they are without judgement, and a willingness to assist them in any way we can, which is why we include it with compassion. Many of us are also unkind to ourselves, putting ourselves down on every occasion, refusing to allow any softness or gentleness to creep in. It is so much easier to self-flagellate than to cut ourselves some slack when things are not working out in life.

If you can learn to embrace kindness, others will flock to connect with you emotionally. You will also discover new insights into yourself, which will make you a more rounded, skilled emotional connector. We will explore later how to develop this skill.

Gratitude

Much has been written about the importance of developing the personal skill of gratitude, and many individuals have discovered that there is much to be gained by practising it in their lives. I do not intend to explore this subject in detail, as others have done so before me. I would like to discuss, however, its role in emotional connection.

There is so much about life, as we have already stated, that is brutal, raw, back-breaking, unfair and at times seemingly hopeless. The recent Covid-19 pandemic brought much of this to the surface. Yet, life at its essence has a wondrous, hidden beauty and thankfully is filled with good things, joy and periods of happiness. Otherwise, it would seem intolerable to many of us.

We can all relate to the automatic tendency of our emotional brain to focus on the negative aspects of what is going on in our lives at a particular moment in time. This is an evolutionary consequence of how we developed as human beings. All of this negativity is, however, not good for our emotional health, as we can tend to look at life through a dark veil, sometimes obscuring the wonderful things that are happening to us at the same time.

Gratitude can be seen as approaching life with a completely different attitude, one that looks instead for the positive things going on in our lives at that moment in time. This of course requires a complete change of perspective, something that most of us have to actively work on. It is more about seeking out what is positive in our lives – those small, wonderful things that we often take so much for granted. This can range from personal relationships with our children to recognizing and rejoicing in Mother Nature in all of its glory. It requires us to be more consciously mindful of such positives in our lives and take pleasure in them.

Gratitude is not about ignoring the difficult, often stressful and challenging aspects of life. That would be both foolish and unrealistic. Rather, it is about identifying that amidst these trials and tribulations that affect us all, there are many simple, everyday positive things that we can all rejoice in and be thankful for. Many religious and spiritual disciplines have incorporated gratitude into the everyday lives of their followers over the last few thousand years but nowadays it is recognized that there are huge psychological benefits to absorbing this positive emotion and attitude into our everyday lives.

Those who practise gratitude have been found to experience the following benefits:

- An enhanced sense of contentment and wellbeing
- Improved sleep patterns
- More robust immune systems
- Increased levels of the feel-good neurotransmitters serotonin and dopamine
- Improved quality of personal relationships
- Decreased levels of stress and anxiety
- Increased levels of mood and less depression
- Feeling more positive and optimistic
- A strengthening of positive neural circuits in the brain associated with happiness and self-fulfilment.

If we had a tablet or supplement that promised to produce the above positive benefits, it would be sold out immediately. Yet all of us have the potential to shift away from our natural tendency to be negative, pessimistic or self-judgemental and embrace instead an attitude of gratitude.

Gratitude also has an important place in our everyday emotional connections. We can tend to bring the more negative side of ourselves into routine everyday social interactions and this can have a flattening effect on such conversations. If, however, we were to approach both life and such interactions with a sense of gratitude, much would change. Both you and the conversational interaction could now be filled with a greater sense of lightness, joy and hope for the future. This is why this personal skill is so critical. Later we will explore how you can introduce gratitude into your life.

Banishing Frustration and Hurt

There are few more damaging emotions to successful emotional connection than frustration and hurt. These emotions and the unhelpful thinking and behavioural patterns that go with them can be poisonous to effective communication. Maybe you can see some traces of these emotions in yourself and, if honest, admit that they are not helping you in your life?

Frustration is one of the most underdiscussed and underrated of all of our unhealthy, negative emotions and more common amongst us than we might care to admit. While all of us will obviously become frustrated with events in life from time to time, some of us have developed unhealthy persistent thinking patterns that continuously drive this emotion, which often appears when communicating with others.

Underlying frustration is a belief that one should not have to suffer discomfort or disturbance, and that situations, people, and indeed life itself on occasion should change to suit us! We each require a healthy sense of humour in relation to ourselves and life in order to challenge this emotion and belief. It is often our behaviour, however, that can lead us into networking difficulties when this emotion is triggered.

You may become more irritable and short with others if they do not see matters through the same lens as you. All of your verbal and non-verbal cues are giving out the same message: 'don't mess with me'. To the person communicating with you, this can be extremely disconcerting as it triggers their social brain to back off and remove themselves from the discussion, or, even worse, to get into an argument with you. This is the polar opposite of what good emotional connection should be all about.

There is usually a further casualty, if frustration is one of your go-to emotions, and that is emotional empathy. Rarely do you discover someone who struggles with frustration and yet oozes empathy. The two simply do not mix well together. This is especially important in business and in the world of personal relationships. If you wish to become more effective in relation to your communication skills, you are going to have to identify and manage your frustration levels if present.

Hurt can be even more damaging. Underlying this emotion is an often deeply held belief that other people and life itself are treating us unfairly and subsequent behavioural responses become corrosive. We become hypersensitive, irritable, prickly, lash out verbally or go into sullen silences. Once again, our verbal and non-verbal cues are sending out powerful messages that tend to push others away when this emotion is triggered during routine social interactions. We also tend to allow hurt to grow legs. This means that the longer things go on, the more hurt builds up in our lives, the more it intrudes into our ability to smoothly network with others. We can find ourselves isolated, lonely and bitter and struggle to hold on to friendships and relationships or to be truly effective in the workplace.

If you can relate to the above, it is essential to develop some new personal skills or techniques to deal with these emotions.

These then are the personal development skills so essential to achieving your objective of becoming an effective communicator. If you can identify some gaps in your own personal development skills, it is well worth skilling up in those areas. In the next chapter, we will explore how best to do just that.

12. How to Improve Your Personal Development Skills

In this chapter, we are going to examine how you can improve your personal development skills. Once again, there may be some parts of greater relevance to you than others, and you may wish to focus more on these sections. If so, then that is absolutely fine. The important message is that improving such skills can be a game-changer for many struggling with emotional connection.

Skill One: How to Develop Self-Acceptance

In the previous chapter, we discussed the importance of self-acceptance or how to be comfortable in your own skin, and its importance in relation to emotional networking. If this is an area of life that you have been struggling with, I recommend the following exercises to assist you in developing this skill.

Personal Development Skills: Rating Observational Exercise

Your first task is to ascertain where you stand on what I call the Rating Scale. On a sheet of paper, draw a straight line. At one end of the line, write 1 and at the other, 100. Now rate yourself as a human being between 1 and 100, with the former being useless and the latter fantastic. Having marked the score for your personal rating, now mark where you believe others would rate you. Next, imagine you had made a major error at work or were informed that there was a rumour going around that you were a poor parent. With each of these situations, where would you now rate yourself on the scale? Then, mark where you think others would rate you on being given this information.

The results of the first part of this exercise will impart some important information about yourself:

- **If your personal rating was under 30** then you may have a very low opinion of yourself. This often occurs when you feel emotionally or clinically down.
- **If between 30 and 50**, your view of yourself is not as negative, but suggests that you are still uncomfortable with yourself in many situations.
- **If between 50 and 90** you are falling into the large group where most people will reside. In general, you feel reasonably comfortable with yourself in most situations.
- **If between 90 and 100** you belong to the group of high raters, and this can mean you put major pressure on yourself in many situations. This group is often associated with perfectionism and fear of failure. If you belong here, you may tend to become anxious or frustrated if not achieving the levels you feel you should be attaining.

Reviewing your assessment of what others think of you can also be revealing. If the 'others' rating is extremely high, you may constantly feel under pressure to match up to other people's perceived high expectations. This can also lead to you becoming anxious. If extremely low, this may suggest that others do not think much of you, so you may be prone on occasion to feeling depressed or ashamed. Once again, most people mark themselves comfortably between the two extremes, assuming others have a reasonable opinion of them.

Now for the results of the second part of this exercise. How many 'changed' their rating when asked to visualize the situation where they made an error at work or were considered a poor parent? My own experience from performing this exercise over many years is that some will mark their self-rating down but not their 'others' rating. The majority will mark down both.

There is of course a major flaw in the above exercise in that it is assuming that you as a human being or person can be rated at all! Yet this is what most of us are doing in real life, every day of the week. Suppose I asked you 'On what grounds, or using what scale, did you apply these ratings to begin with?' Most of us, on reflection, are forced to admit that we cannot answer this question. In practice, no such scale exists. It becomes more complex. Suppose I put three of your children, family members or friends in a row on the couch, requesting you rate them as human beings, each against each other, detailing the grounds on which you have awarded your scores. You would immediately rebel. How can I rate Susan my daughter over Sean my son, for example? They are both completely different, unique, special human beings, and you would be right to refuse to compare one to the other.

One could ask why this is the case. It is because of the wonderfully individual nature of every human being. Each of us is a marvel created by our unique genetic code and individual upbringing. All of us are special, unique and totally undefinable. There is, therefore, no scale or book to measure our worth as human beings. Yet we as human beings constantly fall into the trap of believing that people can be measured by either ourselves or others.

What you are actually doing when playing this rating game is merging who you are with what you do, in terms of your actions or behaviours (which include your skills and talents), and this is so destructive to your mental health and wellbeing. You should be embracing the more radical idea of accepting yourself unconditionally, irrespective of all other factors.

This rating exercise is important, however, as it will give you an idea of whether you tend to do a lot of self-rating if things are not going your way and how much value you are placing on what others think of you. This is your first step on the journey towards unconditional self-acceptance.

Personal Development Skills: Exercise One

You are now ready to take on the task of developing the skill of attaining unconditional self-acceptance. As discussed in the previous chapter, this implies that you cease rating or measuring yourself as a person. It also implies that you cease accepting personal ratings of you by other people in your life. What this means in practice is that you accept yourself as the wonderfully unique, special person that you are, while understanding that you are entitled to analyse and rate your actions, skills and talents, as indeed are others. To do this, you will have to clearly separate who you are as a person from the success or failure of your actions, skills or talents. This is quite a difficult task to accomplish, but those who do so will reap the benefits for life. As discussed in the previous chapter, you will have to combat your arch enemy, namely your pathological critic, if you wish to develop self-acceptance. To achieve this objective, I suggest you perform the following exercise.

For one week and onwards carry a notebook around with you. Whenever you find yourself rating yourself negatively, write down the trigger. Typical examples might involve:

- Somebody at work, or a family member or friend, criticising something you have said or done
- Making a mess of a task or failing at a critical task
- Not getting a job or receiving an expected promotion
- The breakup of an important personal relationship
- Having a row with someone you love.

When free to do so, write down on a sheet of paper what the pathological critic is telling you at such times – for example, that you are a failure, or are useless, or worthless. Then, on that paper (which allows your rational brain to overrule your emotional brain), challenge what the pathological critic (PC) is telling you as follows:

Suppose the comment or rating is that you are 'useless'. You should now dispute this on paper by querying it. What does this really mean? Can I or indeed any human being be defined as 'useless' or of 'no value'? Am I simply rating myself as a person rather than rating how useful or not I am at a particular task or activity? Are we all not useful at some skills, e.g. cooking or gardening or playing music, versus useless in other areas such as public speaking or solving problems around the house, for example?

The great advantage of the latter of course is that you can work on those practical skills that you are not so proficient with. By challenging your PC in this way, you will discover that its power begins to diminish and that you learn to become more pragmatic and realistic about yourself.

Suppose the comment or rating suggests that you are a 'failure' and you wish to dispute this on paper; you might ask similar questions. What does the term success or failure really mean in real life? Can I or indeed any human being be defined as either a success or a failure as a person? Would it not be more accurate to describe how successful or not I am at a particular task or activity in life? How often do we all fail in many areas of life and is this not how we learn as human beings? Is not the greatest failure in life not to get back up and try again? Once again, your PC would like you to believe that it is you, the person, who is the failure, rather than a task or goal that you have set yourself, and it is this fallacy that you must challenge on paper as above.

The same exercise applies to other forms of self-rating emanating from your PC, suggesting you are abnormal, worthless, weak, unlovable or indeed any other similar term. In each case, you challenge the rating as above.

Over time, with the application of this exercise, you will notice yourself becoming increasingly self-confident and much more realistic about yourself and life. You will also find yourself feeling increasingly comfortable with yourself and others in social interactions as a result.

If you struggle in the area of self-acceptance with the tendency to become distressed or bothered by what other people think of you (which underlies the emotion of shame), then during the same week and onwards, challenge this false negative perception as follows:

Whenever you find yourself rating yourself negatively, based on what you perceive as the negative judgements of others, write down what you believe those assessments to be. You will fairly quickly notice that these judgements seem to be quite similar to the PC comments discussed above. In other words that others think that you are 'weak', 'a failure', 'useless', 'weird' and so on. This is because when we allow others to rate us as a person, it is as if we are loaning out our PC to others to beat us up with – not a healthy thing to do.

Once again, on paper, when free to do so, challenge these negative assessments in exactly the same manner as above. Can a human being be rated as a failure, useless, worthless, weak and so on? The answer is clearly no. Can you, like every other human being, mess up in relation to your actions, skills or talents? Of course you can, but you cannot be rated or judged or measured as a person or human being based on how successful or not you are in these areas. This is because all human beings, as already discussed, are totally unique and special.

In this manner, you slowly but surely begin to separate who you are as a person from your actions, skills and talents. If people want to have a discussion about the latter, they are free to do so, but you are not obliged to accept their assessments in these areas if you do not feel they are correct or justifiable.

This is a wonderful exercise for those who struggle in social interactions, constantly believing that the other person is judging or rating them all the time and that such judgements are invariably negative. Imagine if you no longer cared what their judgements were, being completely comfortable with yourself. It is a great place to be, and people will really envy you the self-confidence that flows from this. You will become the go-to person for emotional connection.

Skill Two: How to Apply Humour to Social Interactions

Previously, we examined the importance of having a sense of humour about ourselves and life while engaging in social interactions. We explored how humour can assist us to overcome obstacles that might arise during such conversations. How it often makes it easier to navigate difficult topics. How it can assist us to get messages across, without going into too much detail, which might be otherwise unhelpful.

But is it possible to improve your skills in this area? Is not humour completely individual, even cultural in nature? Are not some of us more at ease with introducing humour into networking, while others find this process more challenging? Are there also many situations where humour would seem completely inappropriate?

While all of the above observations are indeed true, this does not preclude you from improving your skills in this area and, in the process, your emotional networking skills. For those of you who would like to do just that, I recommend the following exercise.

Personal Development Skills: Exercise Two

All of us will regularly find ourselves in multiple social and working scenarios, where we may have an opportunity to introduce humour into the situation. **For one week, in each of these situations, if felt appropriate, try to lighten the atmosphere by introducing some gentle comic or ironic comments and observations into the conversation.** The ideal starting place is to make some good-humoured self-deprecatory observations about yourself. This will immediately get across some simple emotional connection messages. Firstly, that you are not taking yourself too seriously and are well able to poke fun at yourself. This means that you will seem more human and genuine to the other person, as they will often see themselves in some of your comments, but be too embarrassed to admit to them. Secondly, it suggests that you are comfortable in your own skin, a trait so many envy. Thirdly, it allows the other person the time and space to relax into the conversation, as they will not feel as if they have to be on guard for fear of saying something that might upset you.

One essential component of this exercise is that you must ensure that you apply humour more to discussing situations or topics that arise during the conversation, rather than to discussing individuals. The latter is fraught with the risk of personally denigrating others not present to challenge you. The only exception of course being yourself, as discussed above. If you are discussing someone's cooking skills, for example, a humorous comment that 'you should see mine in action' immediately sets the scene.

There will be other occasions, either at work or during a personal relationship encounter, where you find tension levels rising, as differences of opinion rise to the surface. Sometimes, this can be an ideal time to introduce a gentle humorous comment into the mix, ideally about yourself, to defuse the situation. There is nothing like a good laugh, as you will discover while performing this exercise, to clear the air and allow both parties to reset the conversation. It can defuse tension and high emotions, allowing instead a more solution-focused approach to be adopted by both parties.

If you really struggle to perform this exercise, try writing down some simple good-humoured bantering comments, ideally about yourself, and, when you get an opportunity, introduce them into conversation. The key is self-acceptance, as this will allow you to cease taking yourself too seriously. This makes it so much easier to introduce humour in social interactions. It can also be useful to observe others who are comfortable in this area and see how much you can learn from them.

The key word here is practice. Like driving a car, or riding a bicycle or learning a new language, it is constant repetition, trial and error and an acceptance that failure will be a part of the process that will help you to win the day. Bit by bit, you will become increasingly comfortable with using humour in this manner, until it eventually becomes second nature.

Skill Three: How to Practise Kindness

Another really empowering personal development skill is introducing kindness into your interactions with others. This is an attribute that our social brains powerfully respond to, when encountered in others. People who demonstrate kindness are more attractive to us in emotional connection situations. There is an instinctive feeling, when one encounters it – this is a person I can trust, do business with, or want to know better. There is often an aura around such people. They frequently do not talk about their acts of kindness. Yet how they behave and act around others, or how they describe others, are often signposts to the goodness that lies beneath. There is something beautiful about the concept that if you have nothing good to say about someone, say nothing at all.

We can all work on our kindness levels. If you do decide to do just that, there will be two winners: you personally, and those to whom you apply that kindness. If you are interested, I suggest the following exercise.

Personal Development Skills: Exercise Three
For one week I want you to firstly practise kindness in all of your dealings with others. Every conversation or social interaction will be a potential situation for you to do just that. Start by being kind to yourself, especially while talking to others, unless doing so with good humour.

Then consciously focus on the other person, only seeing their more positive side and blocking out any preconceived faults or failings that they might have. This is harder to do than one might think. Focus also on showing them kindness in the little ways that are so important. It might be offering some advice to someone who really needs it or taking those few extra moments to spend time with someone who seems lonely or distressed. It might involve offering to do some simple chores for someone who is struggling with illness, either mental or physical. It could mean standing up for someone who is vulnerable. It might mean never discussing anyone else negatively during a conversation. It could mean sending a text or making a call to someone who really needs it. The list of possibilities is endless.

It might mean listening more to the person who drives you mad, but who has their own underlying issues or problems. It might mean listening attentively and trying to assist a parent who is really struggling with a difficult adolescent or helping someone practically whose family member has dementia.

It could be connecting with someone who is struggling to get to a cancer clinic and driving them there. If a senior citizen is alone and isolated, it could mean doing some shopping for them. It could be just making those crucial cups of tea and sandwiches for visitors to the house of someone who is grieving the loss of a loved one during a wake. It might be taking someone younger and inexperienced under your wing at work, as you sense that they are struggling emotionally and practically. Once again, life will throw up multiple opportunities to practise kindness.

If you practise kindness, the positive effect on you as a person and on your skills as an emotional connector will increase exponentially. You will be a deeper, warmer, less judgemental and more fulfilled human being. You will also be someone whom all of us will instinctively feel like being with. A genuine emotional communicator.

Skill Four: How to Practise Gratitude

We discussed earlier the importance of practising gratitude in our lives and how it could benefit our emotional connection. Like kindness, gratitude is not something that most of us practise routinely. Rather, it is a skill that we have to nurture and grow. Most of us, however, really struggle with this, as it goes against our natural tendency to seek out the more negative aspects of the lives we lead. If you belong to this group, you may find the following exercise to be of some assistance.

Personal Development Skills: Exercise Four

There are two parts to this exercise, the first relating to practising gratitude in your everyday life and the second to applying what you learn to emotional connection situations.

To practise gratitude in your everyday life, for one week and onwards, practise writing down, every day, five things that you feel especially grateful for. It could be that you had a lovely interaction with one of your children, a special night out with your partner, an especially beautiful walk in the forest with the person you love, or that you still have a job, when many around you are losing theirs. It could be that you are grateful for your good health or having a roof over your head. It could be that you are grateful simply to be alive or are happy with the job you are doing or the team you are working with. You might write down how grateful you are to the scientists who develop the Covid vaccines or to the frontline staff who sacrificed so much to keep others well. The list of possibilities is endless.

If you keep up this exercise long-term, you will notice how you are gradually beginning to focus more on the positive aspects of your life and less on the negative ones, which will always be with you, no matter what. It takes a lot of conscious effort to do this at the beginning as it will feel strange. Over time, however, it will become an automatic thing for you to do, to seek out and give priority to those parts of your life for which you now feel grateful.

To practise gratitude in your emotional communications during the same week and onwards, try also introducing the philosophy behind gratitude into every social interaction you have.

Consciously focus on speaking about the areas of life for which you are grateful. Try to speak less about the more negative aspects and more about the positives. The brain can only really focus on one area at a time, so the more time spent on the latter, the less will be spent on the former. You will notice how others will instinctively begin to do the same, as you have subtly changed the direction of the conversation. It will be clear non-verbally that you are not just talking about gratitude, but living it in your life, and this can have a powerful effect on others. They will look forward to future social interactions as a consequence. Add in self-acceptance, a sense of humour and kindness and you are close to becoming a much sought-after emotional connector.

Skill Five: How to Banish Frustration and Hurt

As we discussed previously, there are few more damaging emotions to successful emotional connection than frustration and hurt. These can really impede much of the good work that you have done so far. It is essential, therefore, if you can relate to either of these two common emotions, to develop new ways to challenge them, otherwise you will struggle to become an effective communicator. The following exercises may be of some assistance in this regard.

Personal Development Skills: Exercise Five (a)

At the heart of frustration is an underlying belief that you should not have to experience discomfort and that situations and life must change to suit you. We call this low frustration tolerance, where you desire long-term gain but also seek to avoid short-term pain. You desire everyone else to change, but not yourself. This is usually accompanied by an unhealthy suite of behaviours as previously discussed such as being hypersensitive, irritable or sullen with others. It is this latter that causes such difficulties with our networking with others. If you can relate to this, I recommend this exercise to assist you.

It has two parts; the first relates to how you reduce your frustration levels to begin with, and the second introduces what you have learned into your everyday networking.

If you wish to reduce your tendency to respond instinctively with the emotion of frustration and the negative behavioural consequences that follow, then try this. **For one week and onwards, every time that you find yourself becoming extremely frustrated about something, write down the trigger and your responses in your notebook.** Then, write down the following three questions:

1. What is my long-term objective in this situation?
2. What short-term pain am I trying to avoid in this situation?
3. What changes in my thinking and behaviour do I need to make to achieve my objectives in this situation?

Then proceed to answer these three questions as they relate to the situation you are dealing with. What you will quickly notice is that you are usually either trying to dodge some hassle or discomfort, or else expecting either the person or the situation that is frustrating you to change to suit you. These questions turn the spotlight on what you need to do in this situation! This answer will usually be pretty clear: either change something yourself or accept that in this particular situation it will not be possible to do so and come to terms with this reality. It will also become crystal clear that your behaviour in being irritable and bad-tempered with others is not advancing your current situation one whit. I have seen this exercise transform working and domestic lives and heal many ills. Try it and see.

The second part of this exercise will involve you bringing into your everyday networking the lessons learned from above. This can be done concomitantly with the first part in the same week and onwards. **During this time consciously focus on your natural tendency to become irritable, lash out verbally or become bad-tempered if someone during a routine social interaction says or does something that triggers your frustration levels.** You will have to do one of two things. Either excuse yourself and retreat for five minutes for a coffee or bathroom break, or else bite your tongue and work on suppressing this unhealthy behavioural pattern. The former approach can initially be very useful. During the few minutes when you are withdrawn, write down or ask yourself the above three questions and this will assist you to rationalize your emotion more clearly and show you a path out of the situation. Then return with a smile on your face and put what you have learned into practice.

Over time, you will notice how you are building this new attitude and behaviour into your everyday social networking and find it easier and easier to put it into practice. You will notice how you become calmer, solve issues with others during such interactions, and that others, instead of avoiding you, will be more comfortable approaching you over any issue. This can be a game-changer in terms of your long-term emotional connection skills.

Personal Development Skills: Exercise Five (b)

Now let's turn our attention to how best to banish hurt from your life, especially in relation to its corrosive effects on emotional connection. Underlying this emotion is another unhealthy belief that other people and life itself should not be treating you unfairly. This is accompanied by negative behavioural patterns, such as becoming hypersensitive, irritable, prickly or sullen, all so destructive of healthy communications with others. To counteract the above, I recommend this exercise.

To banish hurt, you need to develop a clearer picture of what really happens when you experience this emotion. The following explains this in greater detail.

1. **Hurt is triggered by the irrational belief that others and life should never treat you unfairly.** This is of course a completely impossible demand to achieve in real life, which is innately unfair. Better to believe that you would prefer life not to treat you unfairly, but instead say 'Hello, life', meaning that you have to take life as it is, not as you would like it to be.

2. **Hurt is all about carrying a 'personal' grudge, which is more harmful usually to you than the person towards whom you are aiming the grudge.** This grudge is like carrying a load of rocks on your back for life.

3. **Hurt damages you more than others**, because the behaviours adopted, such as being hypersensitive etc., tend to push others away, deepening your belief that they and the world are out to get you.

4. **You will drop your burden of hurt when you forgive the person, not because it helps them, but because it helps you.** This does not mean that you are not entitled to challenge the person's actions or behaviours and if necessary make them feel the consequences of them.

5. For this to be successful, **you will have to change your negative behavioural patterns outlined above** and also develop the skill of how best to challenge the negative behaviours of others.

To achieve this objective of reducing or banishing hurt, **for one week and onwards carry a notebook around with you and try to become increasingly aware if someone is causing you hurt.** The easiest way to check this is in your behaviour. If for example you have suddenly become hypersensitive, the chances are that hurt has been triggered, and with it the belief that you have been treated unfairly.

Write in your notebook the trigger, your emotional response and your behaviour. Later, on a sheet of paper, analyse what happened. It may be that something somebody said or did triggered the hurt. For example, it might be a work supervisor implying a task was incorrectly carried out, when that is untrue. You now find yourself holding a grudge against them.

Ask yourself, 'Is carrying this grudge helping or hindering my sense of wellbeing?' The answer is usually that it is hurting you more than the person who triggered the hurt. The final question to ask yourself is, 'Is it in my interests to drop the grudge?' Most of us will agree that it is, but do not know how to do so. Let's explore this further.

The easiest way to drop a personal grudge is to separate who you are as a human being from your behaviour or actions. If we consider this further, perhaps it is not the person causing you the hurt, but their behaviour, that is the core issue? They, too, are a normal human being like you, who has messed up in their behaviour. Would this change how you interpret what happened? This brings us back to self-acceptance – we accepted that human beings cannot be rated, but that their behaviour or actions can. In this scenario, you no longer focus on the person as being the problem, but rather on their behaviour.

If you accept this concept, it allows you to drop the grudge against the person, while remaining free to challenge their behaviour. This allows you to formulate, in a non-confrontational manner, how to do just that. By dropping the grudge against the person in this manner, but shifting attention towards their behaviour, you will also prevent hurt growing legs and avoid days of subsequent ruminations and upset.

You can also challenge, on paper, negative behavioural patterns, if you are carrying such a grudge. Is it helpful to become overly sensitive or verbally antagonistic or lapse into sullen moods? If honest, you will accept such behaviours as unhelpful and decide how best to change them.

But how should you progress to challenging another's actions or behaviour as suggested above? I suggest the following approach:

Initially, if you are feeling extremely annoyed and want to lash out verbally, I suggest that you excuse yourself and retreat for five minutes for a coffee or bathroom break, till you feel calmer and have had a chance to collect your thoughts. Then proceed immediately or as soon as possible to challenge the person's actions or behaviours.

Always challenge a person's behaviour in a calm, measured manner, explaining what it was about their behaviour that caused you to feel upset, how their behaviour affected you emotionally. The other person may be genuinely unaware that their behaviour is causing you difficulties. If you don't let them know, why would they change their behaviour? Often, when they are made aware, they will apologise and change.

This approach teaches us to become comfortable standing up for ourselves if another's behaviour is impacting on our lives. If they continue to behave in such a manner, do not be afraid to proceed further. This may involve removing them from your life, informing HR at work, or whatever other steps are appropriate. On some occasions, you may feel it is not worth the effort. The main point to learn is your right to challenge another person's behaviour. Whether you do so or not is your prerogative.

After performing this exercise regularly, you will notice how automatic it will become to deal quickly with issues that would previously have caused you to feel hurt, and about which you would ruminate, often for days. Notice how much calmer you are becoming and how you are no longer carrying grudges and feel so much the better for this.

One useful connection skill here is to return to the importance of having a sense of humour. When you become more comfortable with your understanding of what hurt is all about and how best to manage it, you may begin to notice how sometimes, you are making mountains out of molehills. If however you choose instead to adopt a sense of humour about yourself and your 'real' importance and about the sheer idiocy of 'getting into the ring' over seemingly trivial matters that you previously would have considered 'slights', then matters can improve even further. A simple humorous self-deprecatory observation during such networking social interactions can be more powerful than any other approach. This is because it often neutralizes the other person and the situation, as both people recognize the humour in the situation and stop taking themselves too seriously.

The art of true emotional connection, in relation to banishing the ill effects of hurt, is to know when to use humour, when not to get into the ring and, most of all, knowing what to do when, as will unfortunately occur at times, you do have to challenge the other person's actions, observations or behaviours.

Before we leave this section, let's see what happens to Bobby, Matt and Angel, when all three decide for personal and professional reasons to work on their personal networking skills.

Bobby's Story

Bobby has always struggled with self-acceptance and with that internal self-critical voice, which constantly reminds him of just how much of a disappointment to everyone, including himself, he is. There are no obvious reasons for Bobby feeling like this, as he experienced a happy upbringing, where both parents constantly encouraged and supported their three children in every way and continue to do so. Bobby has also always taken himself too seriously, which is adding to his problems.

As a consequence of his lack of self-acceptance, he constantly finds himself avoiding emotional connection situations as, in his mind, they are just opportunities for others to see the flaws he sees in himself. This is causing difficulties in both his workplace and new relationship.

Bobby, now in his late twenties, through hard work and a series of lucky breaks has landed the job of his dreams as a designer.

On the way, he has met Zara, a much sought-after model. He is smitten by her good looks and warmth but, as he admits to a close friend, he feels like an impostor. She is simply, in his mind, out of his league. He does his best to dissuade Zara from being with him, as a girl of her stunning looks could do better.

She however has fallen for this silent, self-deprecatory guy, a rare gem in an industry filled with large egos. She constantly re-assures Bobby that she is not going anywhere, that she has found the person she is looking for. Despite this reassurance, Bobby continues to feel that he is not good enough for her, and it is causing difficulties in their relationship.

His poor self-image is also causing difficulties at work, where his unease in networking situations is coming across to others as him seeming aloof and stand-offish, and this is not going down well. He also tends to avoid connecting with others, whom he feels are more talented and important than he is. He believes internally that he is an impostor, both at work and within his relationship. Bobby is doing his best to present an image to the world, that he is completely in charge of everything, while inside he is crumbling.

Thankfully, Zara, who has had her own struggles with negative self-image in the past, recognizes many of the signs, and per-suades Bobby to attend a therapist whom she herself has visited previously. She reveals how her own image difficulties had led to a brief brush with an eating disorder. How, on occasion, when her Instagram pictures were showing her off as a healthy, stunningly dressed, confident young woman, in reality she was at the same time curled up in a chair at home, crying and wondering how she could go on. These admissions shock Bobby, who now realizes that he is not the only one suffering from a poor sense of self. If Zara is brave enough to tackle her issues, maybe it is time for him too to seek assistance. This proves to be one of the best decisions of his life.

Several weeks later, he begins to see Jenny, a warm, empathetic therapist, and someone with whom Bobby immediately feels comfortable. After a long discussion, it becomes clear that his main issues lie in the world of self- and others' rating. Jenny asks him to perform the Rating Observational Exercise (page 205), and neither are surprised at the results. Not only does Bobby constantly rate himself down, for the smallest of reasons, but he also assumes that others too are rating him in a similar manner.

Jenny then challenges him as to whether human beings can indeed be rated at all, either by themselves or by others. What are the criteria for doing so? Are all human beings not unique, special, individual and incapable of being measured, judged or rated? This is an eye-opener for Bobby, who has spent his whole life doing just that. They agree, however, that it is completely reasonable for him to rate or assess his actions or behaviours or indeed his skills or talents, and for others to do likewise.

Bobby begins at last to understand the difference between rating himself as a person versus rating his actions. Jenny elaborates that, when struggling with a poor sense of self, we are falling into the trap of measuring ourselves as a person, depending on the success or failure of such actions, skills or talents. A most unwise decision! But why, Bobby asks, has he fallen into this trap?

This leads to a discussion on the importance of his internal pathological critic (PC) and how this is often formed in childhood and adolescence. How this critical voice is the origin of his current rating difficulties, and the most likely source of his false belief that he as a person is worthless, useless and a failure. How this same voice can be relentlessly negative and self-deprecatory, but that it is possible with the assistance of some techniques to challenge this bully.

Bobby is also surprised to discover that sometimes, even in the absence of any upbringing difficulties, it is possible to put pressure on ourselves from a very early age, by assuming that failing in some task or assignment is an indicator that we are a failure as a person. As Jenny explains, human beings are by no means rational creatures, but prone to picking up such false beliefs about themselves and life, often from an early age. Sometimes unfortunately we carry such beliefs into our adult life, and this is what has happened to Bobby.

Jenny also explains how it is the rating game, allied to the negative comments pouring out of his PC, that is underlining his belief that he is somehow an impostor in relation to both his relationship and his new post at work. If they are going to assist him to defeat what she calls the 'impostor syndrome', they will have to challenge the PC and put it back in its box.

She then progresses to discussing the concept of unconditional self-acceptance, where Bobby should learn to accept himself for the wonderful, unique, special human being he is, someone who can never be personally judged, rated or measured by anyone, including himself.

Jenny elaborates that true self-acceptance would also involve accepting that his behaviour, skills and talents could however be rated or measured by others or himself. In relation to the latter, he does indeed have a duty to carry these out to the best of his ability. She says he also must accept that like every human being, he will regularly mess up or get things wrong. This however should never define who he is as a person as this road leads to great unhappiness.

Jenny then asks Bobby to carry a notebook for the following week and onwards. Whenever he finds himself rating himself negatively, he is to write down the triggering event or thought and then later challenge such ratings on paper. If, for example, he is getting some negative thoughts that he is not good enough for Zara or not up to the job at work, he is to write these down and what his PC is telling him. This might be that he is a failure, or useless or worthless or unlovable. He is then asked to challenge such false beliefs on paper (as already discussed earlier in this chapter).

Bobby really struggles with this exercise and drafts Zara in on occasion to assist him in doing so. He does comment, however, when he sees that his PC is telling him, written down in his own handwriting, how vague and nonsensical at times such statements are in practice.

Gradually, he learns to separate who he is as a person from his success or failure in so many areas of life. He no longer sees himself as being worthless, realizing that such a term is meaningless. He finally comes to understand that a human being cannot be a success or failure as a person, whether at work or in a relationship, but that he could only fail or be successful at some task or assignment in life. He learns not only to quieten his PC, but to be increasingly sceptical of its caustic comments. As he shares with Zara, 'It's time to tame the bully.'

With Jenny's assistance, he becomes increasingly comfortable when networking with other people, no longer trying to remain invisible, believing that he is not good enough. Instead, he is now happy to just be himself. If people like or dislike some aspects of his behaviours or talents, that is their prerogative. He is now comfortable with himself as a person. This has an extremely positive effect on his dealings with colleagues and clients.

Most importantly, he has now come to accept that he is simply a fortunate man indeed, to have attracted the love and support of such a special person as Zara. He no longer feels an impostor in the relationship, accepting that it had been his PC trying to wreck his happiness and long-term emotional wellbeing. He is finally 'comfortable in his own skin'.

Matt's Story

Matt hates connecting emotionally with others. For him, it is a self-fulfilling prophecy that usually ends badly. Since his early teens, he has carried with him two destructive, irrational beliefs. The first relates to a belief that people, situations and life itself must change to suit him, to ensure that he never has to suffer any hassle or discomfort. This belief ensures that he lives and breathes the emotion of frustration. The second relates to a belief that people and life should not treat him unfairly. This ensures that the emotion of hurt is also a constant companion.

As a consequence of his frustration and hurt, Matt is not the easiest person in the world to communicate with. Friends, colleagues, even family learn quickly to tiptoe around him, and to be extremely guarded in anything they might say to him. This is because of his behavioural responses when either of these emotions is triggered. He quickly becomes moody, sullen, argumentative, prickly and hypersensitive and, on occasion, lashes out verbally. This, as would be expected, often leads to others becoming irritated or annoyed with him and letting him know how they feel. This only consolidates the beliefs underlying his frustration and hurt.

The source of his emotions lies in his difficult upbringing. His father, who, like Matt, worked as a mechanic, had been a gruff, taciturn man who himself carried a grudge against the system and the world, believing that the former was set up to only favour the better-off. He also believed that it was up to others to change their ways, rather than him. He has passed some of his views on life on to Matt.

His father then died suddenly, when Matt was sixteen. He was devastated at the unfairness of life, that his father, whom he loved and admired, died so young, having worked so hard all his life. His mum, who was equally heartbroken, never recovered, and died five years later from cancer, leaving behind Matt and one sibling, his sister Eileen. She is the only person Matt can really open up to. She understands her brother, even if she finds his behaviour on occasion extremely trying. She takes after her mum, who was of a much sunnier disposition. The death of Matt's mum, again at such a young age, adds to his sense of unfairness about life. Both of his parents are now gone, leaving the two of them bereft.

Matt, in his late twenties, now works in a busy garage. He is single, as few women are prepared to put up with his negative, often caustic, approach to life. Communicating with this man is just too difficult and relationships quickly grind to a halt.

He is an excellent mechanic, however. His boss would like to promote him to be in charge of his section, but is uneasy about the effects that Matt's behavioural outbursts might have on the other mechanics. Matters suddenly deteriorate when several important clients make complaints about his sullen, non-communicative be-haviour. He is called in for a serious chat by his boss, who lays it on the line. If Matt can find some way to change his attitude and behaviour, he will be considered for promotion. If, however, he continues to act in such a manner, his boss will have to regretfully let him go.

This comes as a devastating blow to Matt, who really loves what he does. He has a long discussion with Eileen, also admitting to her that he is feeling very lonely, with his social circle rapidly di-minishing and his romantic life hitting the rocks. She empathizes with his difficulties but suggests that he is going to need some assistance to overcome them. She contacts a therapist friend, Maeve, who agrees to meet up with her brother.

Matt is extremely uneasy about opening up to another person in relation to his current issues, believing that 'real men don't talk about their feelings'! To his surprise, however, he discovers that Maeve is extremely empathetic and easy to talk to. She gradually coaxes from him all the details of his story. How he is lonely and struggling with personal relationships. How he quickly becomes irritable and short-tempered at work. How poor he is at communicating or networking with other people, both in his job and socially. She is especially interested in the relationship he had with his dad and what messages he has absorbed from this relationship. They agree however that, while it is of assistance to understand the background as to why he is feeling and behaving the way he does, it would be more useful to develop new skills to manage these issues. He is now prepared to work with her, while understanding that it is going to be challenging. As Maeve counsels, 'It is hard to shake off bad habits, built up over many years.'

They begin by focusing firstly on his emotion of hurt. Following some discussions, Matt learns that underlying this emotion is a belief that he should not be treated unfairly by others or life. He learns how irrational and unachievable this belief is in real life. How his actions or behaviours such as being sullen, prickly, or argumentative, for example, are a consequence of his hurt, and how destructive these are in his daily life. How these beliefs probably originated from his upbringing but could be reshaped by working on his negative thinking and behaviours. How hurt, when triggered, was all about carrying grudges, against either others or life, and how this was damaging himself more than others.

This leads to an important discussion on the difference between who we are as human beings versus our actions or behaviours and the importance of self-acceptance. As Maeve suggests, it is wiser to drop any personal grudges against others or life, as these are simply damaging ourselves. Better instead to challenge another person's actions, and to do so quickly and without rancour. A much healthier approach.

To practise this approach, Maeve requests that Matt carry a notebook with him for one week and onwards. If he notes that this emotion of hurt has been triggered, often best seen through his behaviour, he is to write down the trigger, together with his emotion and subsequent behaviour. He then has to analyse what has happened and challenge it on paper, by using the techniques already outlined in this chapter. This will involve, at its heart, forgiving the person but challenging their actions if felt to be unfair.

This exercise would also involve challenging Matt's own behaviours if hurt has been triggered. Was his own tendency to become sullen, hypersensitive etc. helping the situation? If not, what changes will he have to introduce into his life, in relation to these actions?

His next task would be to put into practice the messages he learns from the above exercise. Maeve then gives him some advice as to how best to challenge another person's actions if deemed unfair. This approach, detailed earlier, would involve withdrawing for short periods if emotions are high, then challenging the other person's actions in a calm, non-judgemental manner, making them understand their impact on him and making a request that they review them. If Matt practises it regularly, this technique will resolve most potential hurt situations, without letting them grow legs.

Matt, over the following weeks, works really hard on this exercise and begins to see results rapidly. He becomes more pragmatic, now realizing that most people are often careless in relation to their actions or comments, rather than setting out to cause real distress to him or others. He has simply assumed, up to this point, that everyone is out to get him. As he ruefully admits to Maeve, he has to rethink a lot about what actually happens in real life. He also works hard on trying to change his behaviours, ditching the sullen, argumentative approach and replacing it with the healthier one laid out above. Maeve also suggests that he should learn to adapt a sense of humour about many situations, where the issue involved is not worth the trouble of getting into the ring over. Matt finds this suggestion especially useful.

The benefits of his new approach accrue quickly. His mates at work notice the change and how he is communicating so much better, with them and customers. Gone is the surly manner and demeanour. They also notice, however, how occasionally he pulls them up, if something they say or do seems inappropriate, but does so in a calm, non-confrontational manner. The biggest change is that Matt's previously hidden, sardonic sense of humour, something he has inherited from his dad, is now coming to the fore. These changes, when combined, are making communicating and working with Matt a more enjoyable experience for all concerned. His boss is quick to notice the change in atmosphere and how clients are now seeking Matt out, rather than avoiding him. He fulfils his end of the bargain and promotes Matt to head of his section.

He experiences the emotional connection benefits in other areas as well. With both Maeve's and Eileen's assistance, he re-enters the dating scene. He has done so much work on his thinking and behaviour that he is now seeing relationships through a different lens.

He has become softer and more empathetic than before and soon discovers that these qualities are the key to opening up opportunities in this area. He begins to date Laura, who is a nurse working in a local hospital, someone with warmth and empathy, characteristics that his mum had also demonstrated.

He is now ready, with Maeve's assistance, to tackle the one remaining area of his life that occasionally continues to cause him difficulties, namely the world of frustration. Following discussion, Matt learns that underlying this emotion is a belief that he should not have to suffer discomfort or hassle and that situations and life must change to suit him. Maeve describes him as someone who is suffering from low frustration tolerance or LFT, where he wants long-term gain but prefers to avoid short-term pain. How another feature of LFT is that, when life is not going his way, Matt wants everyone else to change, not himself. Maeve believes that he has picked up this belief from his father and has clung on to it, like a limpet, ever since.

They also discuss how his behavioural response when his LFT is triggered is also leading on occasion to difficulties with others. He has already been working on some behaviours outlined earlier but has further work to do in this area.

To assist him to challenge his LFT, in particular his irrational beliefs and unhelpful actions, Maeve suggests that he carry a notebook with him for the following week and onwards. If he notes that this emotion of frustration has been triggered, he is to write down the trigger, together with his emotion and subsequent behaviour. He then has to analyse what has happened and challenge it on paper. This will involve Matt writing down the three questions outlined earlier in this chapter and applying them to the situation that triggered his frustration. These will explore his long-term goal in the situation, what discomfort he is trying to avoid and what changes in his thinking and behaviour he needs to make to achieve his long-term goal.

Matt finds this frustration exercise extremely 'frustrating' as it involves a lot of hassle and disturbance to keep doing it over the following weeks and months. He discovers, however, that the exercise quickly clarifies why he is becoming frustrated in each situation. There is a clear pattern emerging. In every case he is trying to dodge some painful or annoying experience, all the time wanting other people and situations to change, while remaining unscathed himself! He begins to challenge this approach on paper, and discovers that not only is he less frustrated, but problem situations are quickly resolved. Part of this exercise also involves Matt having once again to challenge his tendency to become irritable and argumentative if his LFT is triggered. He works hard to change this unhealthy pattern and it bears fruit. By the end of this period, he has incorporated this whole approach into his life. He notices how much calmer he has become. This in turn transforms further his connection with others at work and socially.

Several months later, following on from the hard work he has put into banishing hurt and frustration from his life, Matt is a new person. Someone he likes a lot more, who can network comfortably with others, who is now at peace with himself. Most importantly, he is still in a relationship with Laura, with both now looking at a long-term commitment. As he happily admits to Maeve, it really has been a case of short-term pain for long-term gain.

Angel's Story

Angel finds herself, in her mid-thirties, alone and lonely. She is a primary school teacher who has suffered from perfectionism and fear of failure all her life. She continually places unrealistic expectations on both herself and others. She has learned some of these traits at the feet of the master, namely her mum, who was also a total perfectionist. Angel also struggles with poor empathy skills, a trait she shares with her dad, who has inoculated her with a belief that the feelings of others should be of little import.

This combination of poor empathy skills, perfectionism and fear of failure has made it impossible for Angel to find a partner. Who could possibly match up to the excessively high standards she has set for herself and others? It is also interfering with her relationships with colleagues and parents of her students, many of whom find her difficult to communicate with or even like.

She shares her difficulties with a close friend, Sinead, whom she respects greatly, as someone who will tell her to her face what she thinks. Sinead doesn't pull any punches. She sits her friend down, letting her have both barrels. Terms like 'selfish', 'cold', 'self-obsessed', 'perfectionism', 'lacking empathy', 'humourless', 'ungrateful' are tossed out. Angel is stunned by her friend's honesty and by this description of herself as someone she simply does not recognize. Do other people really look at her in this way? Who is this monster that Sinead is describing? Surely this description does not equate to who she really is?

Initially, Angel is annoyed with Sinead's brutal assessment, but the longer the conversation continues, the more she comes to accept the truth underlying her friend's observations. She is especially distressed when Sinead suggests that Angel is going to finish up alone and lonely, unless prepared to make substantial changes in her life. Who for example could ever reach the ridiculously high standards that Angel is setting, in terms of personal relationships? Who is going to want to communicate with someone who is a poor listener, lacks empathy and comes across as cold and uncaring? Someone who is taking themselves too seriously and as a consequence seems totally lacking in humour?

A silence develops in the conversation. Sinead, a skilled communicator coming from the world of HR, allows it to grow. It is up to her friend to join the dots and make the next move. Eventually, Angel admits that perhaps much of what her friend is challenging her with is true, but wonders how she can dig herself out of the hole she has created. Sinead then offers to introduce her to Martin, a life coach, whom we met earlier. She has often sought out his services in the past for colleagues who were struggling with emotional connection, finding him to be extremely helpful.

Facing a spectre of long-term loneliness, and honest enough to admit that her close friend is throwing her a life buoy, Angel agrees. It is to prove to be a wise decision.

Martin turns out to be a warm, non-judgemental life coach. Angel finds it easy to reveal to him her intense loneliness, relationship issues, perfectionism, fear of failure, and her obvious networking difficulties. How affected she has been by the honest comments made by her friend Sinead. Martin empathises, offering to assist her to improve her emotional networking skills.

They begin by spending some time on Angel's listening skills, which have always been poor. She has always been someone who hears, but rarely truly listens to others. Martin describes her as a 'passive listener'. Over the weeks that follow, Martin encourages her to carry out some of the active listening exercises laid out in chapter four. This is the beginning of her journey to becoming a skilled emotional networker.

Martin's next task is to introduce her to the world of emotional empathy, and she really struggles with this concept. She has always struggled with the world of emotions. Over time, however, through a combination of better listening skills and intensely focusing on her empathy skills, she begins to understand what real communication between people is all about. Others, especially

Sinead, begin to see the changes that are occurring and encourage her to continue travelling down this path. On the road, she also learns to understand the importance of those subtle non-verbal cues, which up to this point she has been completely unaware of.

The real work begins, however, when, under Martin's guidance, Angel begins to work on her personal life skills. They begin by focusing on her perfectionism, the trait that has caused her so much distress throughout her life to date. Following a long discussion, they trace its origins back to her upbringing and explore the areas of her life where it is causing her so much damage. Angel is now ready to tackle the monster. This will involve her challenging the false belief that she as a human being must be completely perfect and that if she is not she is a failure. As Martin explains, if she hopes to overturn this unhelpful belief, she will have to challenge both elements of it. The first being that she must be completely perfect in all aspects of her life.

Following discussion, she comes to accept that neither she, nor anyone else she encounters in life, can be absolutely perfect in any area. It is simply an unrealistic expectation, which she is placing on both herself and others. They agree that the consequences of this belief are that Angel is spending her time constantly seeking out imperfections in both herself and others. This is damaging her personally and damaging her capacity to engage with and network effectively with others. Angel now understands that by only seeking out imperfections in herself and others, she has become completely intolerant of anyone exhibiting them. This is to be the major insight that will transform her life. She vows to change this negative pattern. To assist her, Martin gives her some simple exercises. Firstly, he suggests that she notes in a diary over the following weeks and months situations where she was looking for absolute perfection or focusing only on imperfections in herself or others. She then has to challenge this demand on paper. Secondly, he suggested that she get someone at home to mess up a room in her house a few times a week and that she would have to live with the chaos. Lastly, he requested that she mess up something in her appearance daily for four weeks and have to live with the imperfections created for the duration of the day.

Angel finds these exercises incredibly challenging, but slowly over the next few weeks begins to see the effects of her hard work paying off. She notices how she becomes increasingly tolerant of imperfections in herself and others. She also learns to accept that if she waits till everything is perfect before beginning a task, it will never get done. Instead, she forces herself to challenge her stubborn tendency to procrastinate. She also now accepts that 'good enough' does not mean perfect, and that perfection as a concept is both unhealthy and realistically unattainable. The benefits that accrue as a result are amazing. As she comments to Sinead, it is as if a weight is suddenly lifted. No longer is the monster perched on her shoulders.

Concomitantly, Angel begins to challenge her false belief that she is a failure if not absolutely perfect. Angel admits to Martin that her whole life to date has been impaired by a deep-seated fear of failure. How she so often procrastinated due to this fear. How it prevented her from taking risks, especially in relation to personal relationships. How she never believed she was good enough.

Martin, to assist her in challenging this false belief, suggests some exercises to develop her unconditional self-acceptance, something with which she has always struggled. She has never been fully comfortable with herself as a person. She could only accept herself, and indeed others, if they were perfect. She has always believed that she was instead a failure as a person. This lay at the root of much of her unhappiness. She has always been hard on herself and applied the same principles to others. Over the weeks and months that follow, Angel challenges this false belief on paper, going to war as a result with her pathological critic, which is constantly telling her that she is a failure, especially if something in her life is not perfect. Slowly but surely with the assistance of these exercises, however, she puts her inner critic in its box.

The changes that occur as a result assist her to become kinder to herself and others, something that Martin also greatly encourages. As he explains, if Angel is to progress, she will firstly have to learn to show kindness and compassion towards herself. To accept that she is not perfect, will make mistakes and is, like the rest of humanity, fallible. She will also, in time, have to practise kindness and compassion in her everyday dealings with others with whom she will be communicating. Angel, as a consequence, finds herself becoming softer and gentler with both herself and others, discovering the fruits of this change to be transformative.

She also begins to practise another skill, which Martin discusses, namely, that of gratitude. She writes down at the end of each day five things that have occurred during the day to be grateful about. She finds this process extremely positive.

Several months later, Angel has finally moved out of the caterpillar stage of personal development and transformed into a butterfly. The effects on her working and relationship life are transformative. Those who have known her are astonished with the new Angel, someone they barely recognize. Someone who listens intently during conversations, who shows empathy, and is softer, warmer and gentler. More importantly, someone who is now comfortable in their own skin, who no longer seeks out absolute perfection, accepting that both she and others can only do their best. At work, as a consequence, her relationships with colleagues and parents of her students blossom, with both now seeking out her advice and counsel, instead of avoiding her as before. She now shares some of the positive messages she has learned with the children in her class, to great effect.

However, it is the impact of the above changes on her personal relationships that proves to be the most extraordinary. With Sinead's assistance she re-enters this world and, after a period of time, meets Jimmy, a deputy principal in another school. He is taken with this lovely person, who above all seems genuine and empathetic, traits that he values highly. Jimmy has a wonderful sense of humour and does not take himself too seriously. As he good-humouredly comments, 'If you are looking for perfection here, you are in the wrong place!' In the past, as Angel notes to Sinead, 'I would have run a mile, as all I would have seen were his weaknesses and imperfections. Now, I feel increasingly comfortable with this kind, compassionate man. Who knows where it will go, I am just happy to be with him.' Her loneliness, along with her perfectionism and fear of failure, is now thankfully banished into the wilderness. For this and for so much else in her life, she is now truly grateful.

There is so much to learn from Angel's story. In many ways she captures the essence of true emotional connection. As human beings we connect best with each other when we listen more, talk less, are emotionally empathetic, pick up on the non-verbal cues, accept ourselves unconditionally, stop taking ourselves too seriously, stop demanding that we or others are perfect, show kindness and compassion to ourselves and each other and are grateful for what good things life brings to us. As Angel has learned, it is only when we learn to truly share ourselves with others, when appropriate, that real connections are made. The work we put in to arrive at this space will bear, as she has discovered, much fruit.

CONCLUSION

We have come to the end of our journey of discovery into the amazing world of emotional connection. Hopefully you have discovered the incredible power of this form of human connection. How it differs from business or social-media networking. Its importance to your mental health and wellbeing and how it can change and transform your personal and working relationships. How the soft skills involved in emotional connection differ so much from the hard skills involved in science and technology. How those who attain these soft communication skills are better able to surf the many challenges of life.

On our journey we explored the mysterious world of your social brain, the engine that drives much of the conscious and unconscious communications between human beings. How information flowing in from people you are networking with is being constantly monitored, interpreted and acted upon, often at lightning-fast speeds. How the social brain is significantly affected, not only by whatever verbal information is being processed, but by the non-verbal cues being displayed by those you interact with. How your behaviour is, in turn, greatly influenced by the decisions made by your social brain.

We also investigated the role of your mirror neuron and spindle cell systems and the role of language networks within the brain, and their great importance to how you interpret verbal communications; and how which ear you choose to listen with can have a profound effect on whether you are clueing in to a conversation rationally or emotionally.

With this new understanding of the role of your social brain, we then analysed four key strategic sets of essential life skills that constitute the main elements of successful emotional networking: verbal communication skills, non-verbal communication skills, people-to-people skills and personal development skills. In each case we examined which were the main skills necessary for you to become an effective communicator or emotional connector, why they were so important, and then proceeded to demonstrate just how you can acquire the skill in question, through a series of targeted exercises. And, how these soft skills build on one another to form a communication framework that will stay with you for the rest of your life.

We laid out a simple four-week plan that encompassed you taking one skill at a time from each of the four strategic areas of emotional connection and practising them solely for one week apiece.

If you have persevered and systematically practised this four-week plan and practised many of the skills and exercises laid out in this book, you will indeed become a revered emotional connector, whom others will both be attracted towards and admire. Someone who is comfortable in their own skin, an active listener, interested in other people, empathetic, and above all kind and compassionate to both others and yourself. You will notice that you are less stressed, cope better with adversity, are more emotionally resilient, manage conflict better, smooth over turbulent waters in both your working and personal relationships and are someone who will now be seen as a skilled communicator. You will have arrived. A true emotional connector!

ACKNOWLEDGEMENTS

I would like to start as always, by thanking my editorial team at Orion UK for all their wonderful assistance in publishing this book. I want to say a special thank you to my publishing editor Pippa Wright, who has been so supportive, in relation to this book, and indeed the whole series. I am especially indebted to former senior editor Ru Merritt, for her invaluable support, assistance and advice, all of which greatly enhanced this manuscript; I wish her the very best in her new role. I would also like to say a special welcome and thank you to new editorial director Jessica Duffy for her advice and support in relation to structuring the final text, and also to project editor Georgia Goodall for her invaluable assistance in putting it all together.

I am also indebted to publicist Francesca Pearce in the UK and to publicity director Elaine Egan here in Ireland, and Siobhan Tierney from Hachette Ireland for their assistance, in the PR, sales and marketing areas. What a great team to have as an author!

I also owe a huge debt of gratitude as always to Vanessa Fox O'Loughlin, my agent, who has made this whole project possible.

I am indebted as always to my dear friend and national treasure, Sr Stan, founder of the homeless charity Focus Ireland and

Acknowledgements

The Sanctuary Meditation Centre. It has been an honour to be able to dedicate this book to her.

I send the warmest of thanks as always to my good friend Cathy Kelly (bestselling author and UNICEF ambassador) for her constant kindness and support throughout the years. I so value her and her advice.

I would like to especially thank my dear friend and colleague Dr Muiris Houston of the *Irish Times*, for taking the time to review the text, and for his friendship and support.

I would also like to warmly thank *Sunday Independent* columnist and well-known podcaster Stefanie Preissner, for her support and for taking the time to review the text.

I am also as always deeply indebted to eminent Professor Ian Robertson, Professor Psychology Trinity College Dublin, and psychologist Fiona Doherty for taking the time to review the script and for their constant support and encouragement.

A special thank you to my colleague Professor Catherine Harmer, Professor of Cognitive Neuroscience Oxford, for her constant support and for taking time out of her busy schedule to review this book.

I am also so appreciative of my international colleagues Professor Ray Lam, University of British Columbia, Canada, and Professor Larry Culpepper, Boston University, USA, both of whom have been so supportive and took the time to review this book.

I would also like to thank the *Today With Claire Byrne* radio show, especially Claire herself, together with her wonderful team (the excellent series producer Alistair McConnell, producer Barbara Feeney and so many others) for allowing me and my colleague Ann-Marie Creaven the opportunity to highlight key areas of mental health.

Acknowledgements

I say a special thanks to my sons Daniel and Joseph (and Joseph's wife Sue and my beautiful granddaughter Saoirse) and to my daughter Lara (along with her husband Hans and my two much-loved grandsons Ciaran and Sean) for all their love and support and for keeping me well grounded! We have seen the power of human and emotional connection first hand during these difficult times that have tested all of our resilience. Yet love, as always, has sustained us.

As always, I reserve my biggest thank you for my wife Brenda, whose love, friendship, support, encouragement and, particularly, patience has made this book, and indeed the whole series, possible. You will always have my back, as I have yours. You are my light in the darkness, and truly my soulmate. *'Mo ghra, mo chroi.'* (My love, my heart).

BIBLIOGRAPHY

Introduction

Barry, H.P. (2017). *Emotional Resilience: How to Safeguard Your Mental Health.* Orion Spring, London.

Barry, H.P. (2018). *Self-Acceptance: How to Banish the Self-Esteem Myth, Accept Yourself Unconditionally and Revolutionize Your Mental Health.* Orion Spring, London.

Bekalu, M.A., McCloud, R.F. & Viswanath K. (2019). 'Association of Social Media Use With Social Well-Being, Positive Mental Health, and Self-Rated Health: Disentangling Routine Use From Emotional Connection to Us'. *Health Education & Behavior*, 46(2S) 69S–80S.

Part One

1. Emotional Connection

Allen, K.A., Ryan, T., Gray, D.L. McInerney, D.M., Waters, L. (2014). 'Social media use and social connectedness in adolescents.' *The Australian Educational and Developmental Psychologist*, Vol.31 (1), pp.18–31.

Barry, H.P. (2017). *Emotional Resilience: How to Safeguard Your Mental Health*. Orion Spring, London.

Barry, H.P. (2018). *Self-Acceptance: How to Banish the Self-Esteem Myth, Accept Yourself Unconditionally and Revolutionize Your Mental Health*. Orion Spring, London.

Mousavi, S.V., Ramezani, M., Salehi, I., Hossein Khanzadeh, A.A., Sheikholeslami, F. (2017). 'The Relationship between Burnout Dimensions and Psychological Symptoms (Depression, Anxiety and Stress) Among Nurses.' *J Holist Nurs Midwifery*, 27 (2): 37–43.

Schutte, S., Loi, N.M. (2014). 'Connections between emotional intelligence and workplace flourishing.' *Personality and Individual Differences*, 66:134–139.

2. Your Social Brain

Barry, H.P. (2009). *Flagging the Therapy: Pathways Out of Depression and Anxiety*. Liberties Press, Dublin.

Goleman, D. (2006). *Social Intelligence*. Arrow Books, London

Hertrich, I., Dietrich, S. & Ackerman, H. (2020). 'The margins of the language networks in the brain.' *Frontiers in Communication*, Vol.5 – 519955.

Jerger, J. (2018). 'The remarkable history of right-ear advantage.' *Hearing Review*, 25, Number 1, 12–16.

Murphy, K. (2020). *You're Not Listening: What You're Missing and Why It Matters*. Harvill Secker, London.

Orem, T.R., Wheelock, M.D., Goodman, A.M., Harnett, N.G., Wood, K.H., Gossett, E.W., Granger, D.A., Mrug, S. & Knight, D.C. (2019). 'Amygdala and prefrontal cortex activity varies with individual differences in the emotional response to psychosocial stress.' *Behavioral Neuroscience*, 133(2), 203–211.

Riess, H. (2010). 'Empathy in medicine – a neurobiological perspective.' *JAMA*, 304(14):1604–5.

Riess, H. (2017). 'The Science of Empathy.' *Journal of Patient Experience*, 4,(2): 74–77.

Sim, T-C., Martinez, C. (2005). 'Emotion words are heard better in left ear.' *Laterality, Asymmetries of Brain, Body and Cognition*, 10, Vol.2, 149–159.

Part Two

3. Listening Skills

Bao, D. (2020). 'Exploring how silence communicates.' *English Language Teaching Educational* Journal, 3(1): 1.

Chatzinikola, M.E. (2021). 'Active Listening as A Basic Skill of Efficient Communication Between Teachers and Parents: An Empirical Study.' *European Journal of Education and Pedagogy*, 2(6), 8–12.

Jahromi, V.K, Tabatabaee, S.S, Abdar Z.E. & Rajabi, M. (2016) 'Active listening: The key of successful communication in hospital managers.' *Electron Physician*, 8(3):2123–2128.

Murphy, K. (2020). *You're Not Listening: What You're Missing and Why It Matters*. Harvill Secker, London.

Pfeifer, E. & Wittmann, M. (2020).'Thinking, and Feeling: Variations in the Perception of Time During Silence.' *Frontiers in Psychology*, Vol.11.

Robertson, K. (2005). 'Active listening: more than just paying attention.' *Aust Fam Physician*, 34(12):1053–5.

Rönnberg, J. (2016). 'Hearing with your ears, listening with your brain.' *Observer,* Vol.29 No. 2.

Solka, T. (2004). 'Better listening, it's an active process.' *The Hearing Journal*, Vol.57 (9) 40–41.

Sugimori, E., Shimokawa, K., Aoyama, Y., Kita, T. & Kusumi, T. (2020). 'Empathetic listening boosts nostalgia levels and positive emotions in autobiographical narrators.' *Heliyon*, 6(8) e04536.

Zenger, J. & Folkman, J. (2016). 'What great listeners actually do.' *Harvard Business Review.*

4. How to Improve Your Listening Skills

Caspersz, D. & Stasinska, A. (2015). 'Can we teach effective listening? An exploratory study.' *Journal of University Teaching & Learning Practice*, 12(4).

Murphy, K. (2020). *You're Not Listening: What You're Missing and Why It Matters.* Harvill Secker, London.

Solka, T. (2004). 'Better listening, it's an active process'. *The Hearing Journal*, Vol.57 (9) 40–41.

Zenger, J. & Folkman, J. (2016). 'What great listeners actually do'. *Harvard Business Review.*

5. Conversational Skills

Barry, H.P. (2017). *Emotional Resilience: How to Safeguard Your Mental Health.* Orion Spring, London.

Berthoff, A.E. (2014). 'Homiletic Silence and the revival of conversation.' *The Sewanee Review*, Vol.122, No.4, pp.585–91.

Dores Cruz, T.D., Beersma, B., Dijkstra, M.T.M. & Bechtoldt, M.N. (2019). 'The bright and dark side of gossip for cooperation in groups.' *Front Psychol*, 10:1374.

Edmondson, A.C. & Besieux, T. (2021). 'Reflections: voice and silence in workplace conversations'. *Journal of Change Management,* Vol.21 (3), pp.269–286.

Goldberg, S. (2021). 'The Promise and Pitfalls of Online "Conversations".' *Royal Institute of Philosophy Supplement,* 89, 177–193.

Hereford, Z. 'The art of conversation or improve your conversational skills.' www.essentiallifeskills.net

Latif, N., Barbosa, A.V., Vatikiotis-Bateson, E., Castelhano, M.S., Munhall, K.G. & Nusbaum, H. (2014). 'Movement coordination during conversation.' *PLOS ONE,* Vol.9 (8).

Mills, A., Knight, A. & Burdett, T. (2021). 'Supporting student nurses to develop conversational skills.' *British Journal of Community Nursing,* 11, Vol.26 (11), pp.554–559.

Schwab, J.R., Addis, M.E., Reigeluth, C.S. & Berger, J.L. (2016). 'Silence and (In)visibility in men's accounts of coping with stressful life events.' *Gender & Society,* 30(2):289–311.

Hartung, F.M., Krohn, C. & Pirschtat, M. (2019). 'Better than its reputation? Gossip and the Reasons Why We and Individuals With "Dark" Personalities Talk About Others.' *Frontiers in Psychology,* 10, 1162.

6. How to Improve Your Conversational Skills

Barry, H.P. (2017). *Emotional Resilience: How to Safeguard Your Mental Health.* Orion Spring, London.

Barry, H.P. (2020). *Emotional Healing: How to Put Yourself Back Together Again.* Orion Spring, London.

McKay-Semmler & Semmler, S.M. (2013). 'The art of making conversation: learning the skills small talk.' *Communication and Theater Association of Minnesota Journal*, Vol.40, (1) Art. 6.

Part Three

7. Non-verbal Communication Skills

Asan, O., Kim, S.C., Iglar, P. & Yan, A. (2018). 'Differences in verbal and nonverbal communication between depressed and non-depressed elderly patients.' *Journal of Communication in Healthcare*, 11(4), 297–306.

Barmaki, R. (2016). 'Improving social communication skills using kinesics feedback.' *Proceedings of the 2016 CHI Conference Extended Abstracts on Human Factors in Computing Systems*, (CHI), 86–91.

Bonaccio, S., O'Reilly, J., O'Sullivan, S.L & Chiocchio, F. (2016). 'Nonverbal Behavior and Communication in the Workplace: A Review and an Agenda for Research.' *Journal of Management*, 42(5):1044–1074.

Docan-Morgan, T., Manusov, V. & Harvey, J. (2013). 'When a Small Thing Means so Much: Nonverbal Cues as Turning Points in Relationships.' *Interpersona: An International Journal on Personal Relationships*, 7(1), 110–124.

De Stefani, E. & De Marco, D. (2019). 'Language, Gesture, and Emotional Communication: An Embodied View of Social Interaction.' *Front. Psychol*, 10:2063.

Bibliography

D'Agostino, T.A. & Bylund, C.L. (2014). 'Nonverbal accommodation in health care communication.' *Health Communication*, 29 (6), 563–573.

Dunbar, R.I.M., Robledo, J.P., Tamarit, I., Cross, I. & Smith, E. (2022). 'Nonverbal Auditory Cues Allow Relationship Quality to be Inferred During Conversations.' *J Nonverbal Behav*, 46(1):1–18.

Goldin-Meadow, S. & Alibali, M.W. (2013). 'Gesture's role in speaking, learning, and creating language.' *Annu Rev Psychol*, 64:257–83.

Hall, E.T. (1968). 'Proxemics.' *Current Anthropology*, 9, No.2: 83–95.

Hall, J.A., Horgan, T.G. & Murphy, N.A. (2019). 'Nonverbal communication.' *Annual Review of Psychology*, 70, 271–294.

Hietanen, J.K. (2018). 'Affective Eye Contact: An Integrative Review.' *Front Psychol*, 9:1587.

Ho, S., Foulsham, T. & Kingstone, A. (2015). 'Speaking and listening with the eyes: gaze signaling during dyadic interactions.' *PLOS ONE*, 6;10(8):e0136905.

Jiang, J., Borowiak, K., Tudge, L., Otto, C. & von Kriegstein, K. (2017). 'Neural mechanisms of eye contact when listening to another person talking.' *Social Cognitive and Affective Neuroscience*, 12 (2), 319–28.

Liu, C., Calvo, R.A. & Lim, R. (2016). 'Improving Medical Students' Awareness of Their Non-Verbal Communication through Automated Non-Verbal Behavior Feedback.' *Front. ICT*, 3:11.

Mitzkovitz, C., Dowd, S.M., Cothran, T., et al. (2022). 'The Eyes Have It: Psychotherapy in the Era of Masks.' *J Clin Psychol Med Settings*, 1–12.

Pereira, M., Meng, H. & Hone, K. (2021). 'Prediction of Communication Effectiveness During Media Skills Training Using Commercial Automatic Non-verbal Recognition Systems.' *Front. Psychol*, 12:675721.

Prabhu, T. (2010). 'Proxemics: Some Challenges and Strategies in Nonverbal Communication.' *The IUP Journal of Soft Skills*, Vol.4, No. 3, pp. 7–14.

8. How to Improve Your Non-verbal Communication Skills

Krznaric, R. (2014). *Empathy: Why It Matters and How to Get It.* Penguin Random House, London.

Riess, H. (2010). 'Empathy in medicine – a neurobiological perspective.' *JAMA*, 304(14):1604–5.

Riess, H. & Kraft-Todd, G. (2014). 'E.M.P.A.T.H.Y. A Tool to Enhance Nonverbal Communication Between Clinicians and Their Patients.' *Academic Medicine*, Vol.89(8), pp. 1108–1112.

Vogel, D., Meyer, M. & Harendza, S. (2018). 'Verbal and non-verbal communication skills including empathy during history taking of undergraduate medical students.' *BMC Med Educ*, 18, 157.

Part Four

9. People-To-People Communication Skills

Angelo, E. (2019). 'Managing interpersonal conflict: Steps for success.' *Nursing Management*, 50(6), 22–28.

Bibliography

Bao, Y., Zhu, F., Hu, Y. & Cui, N. (2016). 'The Research of Interpersonal Conflict and Solution Strategies.' *Psychology*, 7, 541–545.

Barry, H.P. (2017). *Emotional Resilience: How to Safeguard Your Mental Health.* Orion Spring, London.

Denault, V. (2020). 'Misconceptions About Nonverbal Cues to Deception: A Covert Threat to the Justice System?' *Frontiers in Psychology*, 11, 573460.

Healey, M.L. & Grossman, M. (2018). 'Cognitive and affective perspective-taking: evidence for shared and dissociable anatomical substrates.' *Front Neurol*, 9:491.

Jenkins, A.C. (2019). 'Empathy affects tradeoffs between life's quality and duration.' *PLOS ONE*, 14(10).

Krznaric, R. (2014). *Empathy: Why It Matters, and How to Get It.* Penguin Random House, London.

Majer, J.M., Barth, M., Zhang, H., van Treek, M. & Trötschel, R. (2021). 'Resolving Conflicts Between People and Over Time in the Transformation Toward Sustainability: A Framework of Interdependent Conflicts.' *Front. Psychol*, 12:623757.

Riess, H. & Kraft-Todd, G. (2014). 'E.M.P.A.T.H.Y.: A Tool to Enhance Nonverbal Communication Between Clinicians and Their Patients.' *Academic Medicine*, 89 (8):1108–1112.

Riess, H. (2010). 'Empathy in medicine – a neurobiological perspective.' *JAMA*, 304(14):1604–5.

Riess, H. (2017). 'The Science of Empathy.' *Journal of Patient experience*, 4,(2): 74–77.

Stietz, J., Jauk, E., Krach, S. & Kanske, P. (2019). 'Dissociating Empathy From Perspective-Taking: Evidence From Intra- and Inter-Individual Differences Research.' *Front. Psychiatry*, 10:126.

Trötschel, R., Hüffmeier, J., Loschelder, D.D., Schwartz, K. & Gollwitzer, P.M. (2011). 'Perspective taking as a means to overcome motivational barriers in negotiations: when putting oneself into the opponent's shoes helps to walk toward agreements.' *J. Pers. Soc. Psychol*, 101, 771–790.

Vogel, D., Meyer, M. & Harendza, S. (2018). 'Verbal and non-verbal communication skills including empathy during history taking of undergraduate medical students.' *BMC Med Educ*, 18, 157.

10. How to Improve Your People-To-People Communication Skills

Angelo, E. (2019). 'Managing interpersonal conflict: Steps for success.' *Nursing Management*, 50(6), 22–28.

Bao, Y., Zhu, F., Hu, Y. & Cui, N. (2016). 'The Research of Interpersonal Conflict and Solution Strategies.' *Psychology*, 7, 541–545.

Barry, H.P. (2017). *Emotional Resilience: How to Safeguard Your Mental Health*. Orion Spring, London.

Barry, H.P. (2020). *Emotional Healing: How to Put Yourself Back Together Again*. Orion Spring, London.

Barry, H.P. (2021). *Embracing Change: How to Build Resilience and Make Change Work for You*. Orion Spring, London.

Docan-Morgan, T., Manusov, V. & Harvey, J. (2013). 'When a Small Thing Means so Much: Nonverbal Cues as Turning Points in Relationships.' *Interpersona: An International Journal on Personal Relationships*, 7(1), 110–124.

Overton, A.R. & Lowry, A.C. (2013). 'Conflict Management: Difficult Conversations with Difficult People.' *Clinics in Colon and Rectal Surgery*, 26 (4).

Riess, H. & Kraft-Todd, G. (2014). 'E.M.P.A.T.H.Y.: A Tool to Enhance Nonverbal Communication Between Clinicians and Their Patients.' *Academic Medicine*, 89 (8):1108–1112.

Sclavi, M. (2014). 'The Role of Play and Humor in Creative Conflict Management.' *Negotiation Journal*, 157–180.

Trötschel, R., Hüffmeier, J., Loschelder, D.D., Schwartz, K. & Gollwitzer, P.M. (2011). 'Perspective taking as a means to overcome motivational barriers in negotiations: when putting oneself into the opponent's shoes helps to walk toward agreements.' *J. Pers. Soc. Psychol.*, 101, 771–790.

Vogel, D., Meyer, M. & Harendza, S. (2018). 'Verbal and non-verbal communication skills including empathy during history taking of undergraduate medical students.' *BMC Med Educ*, 18, 157.

Part Five

11. Personal Development Skills

Barry, H.P. (2017). *Emotional Resilience: How to Safeguard Your Mental Health*. Orion Spring.

Barry, H.P. (2018). *Self-Acceptance: How to Banish the Self-Esteem Myth, Accept Yourself Unconditionally and Revolutionize Your Mental Health*. Orion Spring, London.

Barry, H.P. (2021). *Embracing Change: How to Build Resilience and Make Change Work for You*. Orion Spring, London.

Chamberlain, J.M. & Haaga, D.A.F. (2001). 'Unconditional Self-Acceptance and Psychological Health.' *Journal of Rational-Emotive & Cognitive-Behavior Therapy*, 19, 163–17.

Cotney, J.L. & Banerjee, R. (2019). 'Adolescents Conceptualizations of Kindness and its Links with Well-being: A Focus Group Study.' *Journal of Social and Personal Relationships*, 36(2):599–617.

Day, G., Robert, G. & Rafferty, A.M. (2020). 'Gratitude in Health Care: A Meta-narrative Review.' *Qualitative Health Research*, 30(14):2303–2315.

Duckworth, A.L., Tsukayama, E. & Kirby, T.A. (2013). 'Is it really self-control? Examining the predictive power of the delay of gratification task.' *Personality & Social Psychology Bulletin*, 39(7), 843–855.

Duckworth, A.L., Gendler, T.S. & Gross, J.J. (2016). 'Situational Strategies for Self-Control.' *Perspectives on Psychological Science: A Journal of the Association for Psychological Science*, 11(1), 35–55.

Dunbar, R.I., Launay, J. & Curry, O. (2016). 'The Complexity of Jokes Is Limited by Cognitive Constraints on Mentalizing.' *Human Nature (Hawthorne, N.Y.)*, 27(2), 130–140.

Fryburg, D.A., Ureles, S.D., Myrick, J.G., Carpentier, F.D. & Oliver, M.B. (2021). 'Kindness Media Rapidly Inspires Viewers and Increases Happiness, Calm, Gratitude, and Generosity in a Healthcare Setting.' *Frontiers in Psychology*, 11, 591942.

Huber, G. (2022). 'Putting humour to work: To make sense of and constitute organizations.' *International Journal of Management Reviews*, 1–20.

Bibliography

Layous, K., Sweeny, K., Armenta, C., Na, S., Choi, I. & Lyubomirsky, S. (2017). 'The proximal experience of gratitude.' *PLOS ONE*, 12(7): 0179123.

O'Connell, B.H., O'Shea, D. & Gallagher S. (2017). 'Feeling Thanks and Saying Thanks: A Randomized Controlled Trial Examining If and How Socially Oriented Gratitude Journals Work.' *J Clin Psychol*, 73(10):1280–1300.

Park, S.Q., Kahnt, T., Dogan, A., Strang, S., Fehr, E. & Tobler, P. N. (2017). 'A neural link between generosity and happiness.' *Nature Communications*, 8, 15964.

Sclavi, M. (2014). 'The Role of Play and Humor in Creative Conflict Management.' *Negotiation Journal*, 157–180.

Wong, Y.J., Owen, J., Gabana, N.T., Brown, J.W., McInnis, S., Toth, P. & Gilman, L. (2018). 'Does gratitude writing improve the mental health of psychotherapy clients? Evidence from a randomized controlled trial.' *Psychother Res*, 28(2):192–202.

12. How to Improve Your Personal Development Skills

Barry, H.P. (2017). *Emotional Resilience: How to Safeguard Your Mental Health.* Orion Spring, London.

Barry, H.P. (2018). *Self-Acceptance: How to Banish the Self-Esteem Myth, Accept Yourself Unconditionally and Revolutionize Your Mental Health.* Orion Spring, London.

Barry, H.P. (2020). *Emotional Healing: How to Put Yourself Back Together Again.* Orion Spring, London.

Barry, H.P. (2021). *Embracing Change: How to Build Resilience and Make Change Work for You.* Orion Spring, London.

Bibliography

O'Connell, B.H., O'Shea, D. & Gallagher S. (2017). 'Feeling Thanks and Saying Thanks: A Randomized Controlled Trial Examining If and How Socially Oriented Gratitude Journals Work.' *J Clin Psychol*, 73(10):1280–1300.

Wong, Y.J., Owen, J., Gabana, N.T., Brown, J.W., McInnis, S., Toth, P. & Gilman, L. (2018). 'Does gratitude writing improve the mental health of psychotherapy clients? Evidence from a randomized controlled trial.' *Psychother Res*, 28(2):192–202.

INDEX

adrenaline 36
alcohol 36
Alzheimer's disease 31
amygdala 28, 29, 30, 31, 32, 36, 37, 120
anxiety 2, 8, 10, 26
  brain function and 26
  misreading non-verbal cues 162
  see also social anxiety
Asperger's syndrome 162
autism spectrum 10, 35, 162
avoidant behaviours 26, 36, 108

being yourself, importance of 21, 193, 197–8
bigger picture, seeing 28
body language 65–6, 124–6, 141–3
  during conversation 93–4, 105
  fidgeting 125, 142, 143
  hand gestures 124, 125, 142, 143
  hands on hips 125, 154

harmonizing with verbal messages 93–4, 142
head-tilting 41, 53–4, 55, 63, 64, 125, 142, 143
mirroring 143
negative 36, 47, 93, 101
positive 37, 94
posture 124–6, 141–3, 154
unconscious 94, 125, 142–3
video analysis 141, 143
see also non-verbal communication
boring, describing yourself or others as 78, 79, 95, 106, 109
Botox 121
brain 12–13, 24–41
  amygdala 28, 29, 30, 31, 32, 36, 37, 120
  creativity 27
  language networks 37–41
  limbic system 25–6, 29–32
  neural networking systems 25, 32–5

Index

difficult social situations,
    managing 167–9, 178–80,
    188–90
    careful listening 179
    concerns, validating 179, 189
    humour, using 189, 198, 213
    not making it personal 178
    problem-solving focus 178,
        179, 189
    remaining calm 178, 188–9
    see also frustration and hurt;
        social anxiety
dopamine 36

emotional connection 5–23
    acquired or inherent 6
    both skill and an art 13–14
    businesses and 12
    conscious 12–13
    definition and characteristics 6
    importance and benefits of 7–8
    mental health and 9–10
    neuroscience of *see* brain
    subliminal 12–13
    vs social media 16–20
    young people and 11
emotional resilience 2, 6
emotional self-control 28, 29,
    30
emotional suppression 28
empathy 11, 14, 19, 37, 162–6,
    168, 184–6
    acquired or inherent 163, 186

brain function and 28, 32, 33,
    34–5
cognitive empathy
    (perspective-taking) 159,
    165–6, 173, 174
compassion 11, 166, 193, 199,
    214–16, 240
compassion fatigue 165
emotional empathy 159, 164–5,
    172–4, 186–8, 203, 237–9
enhancing 20, 170–5, 237–8
lack of 166, 186
observational exercise 170–1
positive and negative 163–4,
    171, 187
expressive aphasia 38
extroverts 47, 82, 83–4, 99–100,
    103, 128
eye contact 20, 94, 101, 122–4,
    146
    at the start of conversations
        139, 153
    avoidance 123, 153
    limiting direct eye contact 139
    making genuine eye contact
        137–40, 153
    'politician's gaze' 139
    shifting 139–40, 153
    smiling and 120, 138, 140, 153
    when shaking hands 146

face-to-face communication 1, 7,
    18, 19–20

Index

right PFC 26, 27
ventromedial cortex (VMPFC)
28
primary emotions 30
proxemics 129
see also personal space
psychopaths 28

rational brain 13, 25, 27, 29,
132
reading people 182–3, 184
first impressions 160–1, 176–7,
182–3, 184, 198
see also non-verbal
communication

self-acceptance 11, 193, 194–6,
205–11, 213, 224–9
at ease with admitting errors or
weaknesses 195, 239
challenging your inner critical
voice 196, 210, 228, 239–40
developing 205–11
life story 224–9
non-judgmental 195
observational exercise 205–8
others' rating of you 195, 196,
206–7, 209–11, 226
self-rating 205–6, 207, 226,
227–8
unconditional 194, 196, 208,
211, 227, 239
self-awareness 38, 83, 193

see also personal development
skills
self-judgement 26, 194, 206,
208–9
see also self-acceptance
self-obsession 45, 48, 53, 54, 69,
73, 100
silence, importance of
in conversation 73, 76–7, 87–8,
97–8, 106–7
in listening 55–7, 59, 66–8, 70
smartphones 1, 17, 18
smiling 120, 136, 138
with the eyes 120, 138, 140, 153
Snapchat 17
social anxiety 10, 26, 30, 78, 120
avoidant behaviours 26, 36, 108
engaging in conversation in
a social setting 99–103,
107–11
face-monitoring others 120
life stories 36–7, 107–11
misreading non-verbal cues 30,
162
social brain 24–41, 116, 117–18,
119, 123–4, 127–9, 130, 131,
132, 134, 160, 243
social media 1, 7, 16–20
benefits 18–19
burnout 19
downsides 18, 19
emotional connection and
16–20

272

Index

self-rating game 194
soft skills 14–15, 243
spindle cell network 32–4, 37
stress 2, 8, 9
    amygdala and 30, 36
stroke 38, 121

Teams 18
therapists 22, 35
TikTok 17
tone of voice and pitch 38, 86
touch 126–9, 144–8, 155–6
    cultural and social dimensions 126, 127, 144
    handshakes 126, 127–8, 144, 145–7, 155–6
    harnessing the power of 144–8

hugs and embraces 126, 127, 144–5, 155–6
    kissing 145
Twitter 5, 17

verbal strategies *see* conversational skills

Wernicke's area 38, 40
WhatsApp 18
written word 15–16

young people
    emotional connection and 11
    mental health difficulties 11

Zoom 18
    Zoom fatigue 19

273

ABOUT THE AUTHOR

Dr Harry Barry is a highly respected Irish author and medic, with over three decades of experience as a GP. With a keen interest in the area of mental health and suicide prevention, Dr Barry is the bestselling author of numerous books addressing various aspects of mental health, including anxiety, depression, toxic stress and emotional resilience.

Other life-changing books from Dr Harry Barry

Embracing Change
How to build resilience and make change work for you
From the International No.1 Bestselling Author
DR HARRY BARRY

FROM THE NO.1 INTERNATIONAL BESTSELLING AUTHOR
EMOTIONAL HEALING
How to put yourself back together again
DR HARRY BARRY

How to banish the self-esteem myth, accept yourself unconditionally and revolutionize your mental health.
SELF-ACCEPTANCE
DR HARRY BARRY
THE No.1 INTERNATIONAL BESTSELLING AUTHOR

'Another masterpiece from a cutting-edge expert'
Dr Muiris Houston, The Irish Times
EMOTIONAL RESILIENCE
How to safeguard your mental health
THE BRAND NEW BOOK FROM INTERNATIONAL BESTSELLING AUTHOR
DR HARRY BARRY

TOXIC STRESS
A step-by-step guide to managing stress
DR HARRY BARRY

THE INTERNATIONAL BESTSELLER
FLAGGING THE PROBLEM
A new approach to mental health
DR HARRY BARRY

FLAGGING THE THERAPY
Pathways out of depression and anxiety
FROM THE INTERNATIONAL BESTSELLING AUTHOR
DR HARRY BARRY

'If I were to recommend just one book to read on depression, it would be this'
Carole Miriam Hunt, Sunday Independent
DEPRESSION
A practical guide
FROM THE INTERNATIONAL BESTSELLING AUTHOR
DR HARRY BARRY

THE NO.1 INTERNATIONAL BESTSELLER
ANXIETY AND PANIC
How to reshape your anxious mind and brain
DR HARRY BARRY